SAVE THE
ORANGUTANS

Gerry Huerth

STRATTON
—PRESS—
Publishing Life

SAVE THE ORANGUTANS
Copyright © 2022 **Gerry Huerth**

Stratton Press Publishing
831 N Tatnall Street Suite M #188,
Wilmington, DE 19801
www.stratton-press.com
1-888-323-7009

ISBN (Paperback): 978-1-64895-729-1
ISBN (Ebook): 978-1-64895-730-7

Printed in the United States of America

Sitting in a tree
Orangutan alone
Content to be
The jungle's very own.

This novel takes place in 1995.

CHAPTER 1

EVERY JUNE WHEN the sun reached its summer zenith, Frannie Fortunato would begin preparations for her annual fete; and each year looking around her tiny house, she would yet again be amazed at what had accumulated there. She would resolutely begin tidying up, examining the piles of books and papers and who knows what that had gathered in strategic places since her last year's summer fete.

She started this year with the pile by the sofa: a couple of books that she had read months ago, an electric bill from last October, a well-thumbed-through plant catalogue, and a piece of paper on which a phone number had been scrawled and underlined in red. Well, at least she could throw that out! She crumpled the paper and then straightened the edges of the pile and set off to explore another cache next to her phone. She even dusted all the bric-a-brac, treasures from friends and acquaintances and absolute strangers who continually moved in and out of the orbit of her life.

She loved the sound of that word *fete*—so simple yet so exotic, a sophisticated word full of international mystery and romance that only the initiated could fully understand, such an evocative word, so unlike the very ordinary world that she had long ago eschewed.

She yanked up the Indian batik spread that was draped on the sofa in the living room, walked to the door, stood on the front step, and released an end. As crumbs, paper clips, and a year's worth of dust gently rained out on the grass below, she was sure that this upcoming fete, as usual, would be the most fantastic ever. She would wear that long skirt, the crinkly one covered with flocks of printed birds that startled with her every movement, which was a four-dollar bargain at a garage sale. Of course, she would wear a tie-dyed T-shirt; tie-dye was de rigueur for the particular brand of nostalgia in which she and her circle of friends engaged.

Her fetes were a tradition of sorts—one of those customary rituals that marked her life in lieu of more ordinary calendar events.

This summer, she would top her costume off with a wide floppy hat—a real lawn party hat that she had bought February before when the bridal shop up the street was closing, selling all its paraphernalia for a song.

She stood there on her front steps motionless, gliding through her anticipation until she noticed the spread hanging from her fingertips. Her face twitched in startled disapproval at the intrusion of that mundane obligation hanging from her hands.

Sternly she gave the spread one authoritative shake. It snapped, leaving behind a cloud of dust. Once again, arms holding that multi-colored sail, she resumed her motionless glide caught on the currents of her dreams. She would wear the hat…yes. And what a wonderful hat!

What a prize she had carried home that stark February afternoon, walking along ice-glazed sidewalks; the sun low in the sky at three in the afternoon. A rude wind rushing through the gray buildings and the net of naked trees shoved past her padded steam-huffing form leaving her prize, her hat, flopping in her gloved hands like some ungainly butterfly caught buffeted by winter.

Even under layers of sweaters and jackets and scarves, her eyes peered out excited by the promise of her summer entertainment and that butterfly. Her lips moved slightly, a mere flutter in the darkening privacy of winter, making plans, designing that sunny afternoon to come. Why, she could tie a purple ribbon round the crown of that hat; it would be a purple theme this year.

Of course she would wear her peace button. Where did she put that last summer? She could pin it to the front of the hat. Fabulous—everyone would think it's fabulous! What foresight she had when it came to her entertainments.

She had long since mastered the conjuring trick of breathless anticipation. She had learned that if she concentrated long enough on what she wanted to happen, whatever she longed for would materialize in no time. And if it didn't, at least she was spared some of the rigors of ordinary existence.

She had a way of stirring the prosaic coordinates of life into an exotic stew of her own making. Straight lines and predictable sequences seemed to warp under the influence of her excited imagination. And she could always count on being a hit with her coterie of acquaintances.

Each year, momentarily brimming with nostalgia for their youth, they would converge on Frannie's house of memories to be entertained by her frenzy. Over the years, they watched the gray creep into her frizzy red hair, not that they ever mentioned it to her. She was their sacrifice to the memories of what they had once been.

Each summer, her friend Dodo would say that she looked like an acidhead debutante, and Dodo should know. He had spent his entire twenties in a haze of marijuana, listening to the Grateful Dead and looking forward to his next trip: be it to Taos or to the fantasy-infested frontiers of his mind.

Dwayne (Dwayne—that's what he wanted to be called now), although back then, he was Dodo; and she, Frannie, was DeeDee. He had bestowed that name on her the very first summer of their acquaintance in the basement of her mother's house.

Chips and chip dip between them, he asked her what she wanted to be when she grew up. In a moment of unfortunate self-exposure, she said, "Sandra Dee."

He said, "You've got to be kidding. Sandra Dee! Sandra Dee, Dee!" DeeDee the character was born.

They both walked into the horizon of the peace and love generation—Siamese twins. When their patched-jeaned friends would see them coming, they would all call out like an excited flock of birds, "There's Dodo and DeeDee, Dodo and DeeDee, Dodo and DeeDee." Those two were absolutely inseparable, although no one was exactly sure of the nature of their bond, not that that was a particularly analytical age.

Back then, Frannie may have thought it was a bit unusual that Dodo enjoyed dressing her up, so she had to admit he really did have a flair for it.

He was such a cute boy back then; he spoke with this funny little accent.

Four years before, he had moved with his family from the borough of Queens, New York. Frannie, who had spent most of her pre-Dodo teenage Saturday evenings watching television in her suburban basement, became glamorous at his side even if they were standing out in the middle of nowhere waiting to hitch a ride, and they hadn't showered for days.

Dodo was dead. Long live Dwayne, the very sober twelve-stepped therapist!

Like so many of her guests, Frannie was his last fading memory of those halcyon days of psychedelic bliss. He now wore very neat, preppy clothes, drove a BMW, looked out at the world through tortoiseshell-rimmed bifocals, and of course, he was married to Thomas the lawyer. Although back then, gay marriage was not legal, somehow they did it anyway…leave it to lawyers.

Once a month, Dwayne would interrupt his busy schedule, drive up to Frannie's tiny home, open the two top buttons of his shirt, and grab a hidden pack of cigarettes from his glove compartment, his monthly stolen pleasure.

CHAPTER 2

THAT LATE AFTERNOON in June, the very day that Frannie had begun her fanciful cleaning, Dwayne arrived, pack of cigarettes in the pocket of his recently unbuttoned shirt. The two partners in crime set out on foot from Frannie's home toward downtown, past the run-down apartment buildings and group homes for mentally ill people who bordered her neighborhood. Off they went to the Laughing Cup, more than a coffee shop, a place where people could sit and grow old and fat and shabby and even smoke, a refuge for Dodo and DeeDee and anyone else who landed there.

The two stepped through the smoky doorway. He, a very proper-looking balding gay man whose shirt buttons seemed to be becoming undone, and she, a slightly shriveling, red-frizzed woman with just a little too much lipstick on.

At first, under the pressure of being Dwayne the therapist, he looked around the coffee shop uneasily to make sure none of his clients was present. All clear; the two walked toward the counter—he to order the espresso bomb and she her latte. He had not only given up cigarettes but also caffeine.

With cups of coffee large enough to hold their dreams, they moved on to their accustomed table in the special kind of slow motion that preceded longed-for events. As he sat down, his hand was already inching toward his packet of cigarettes. Frannie sat down too, silently following his lead, afraid that any interruption on her part would halt his metamorphosis back into Dodo.

By the time they settled into their chairs, he was slipping the book of matches from under the cellophane of the cigarette pack, just where he had carefully placed it one month ago. With the solemnity of a high priest, he tapped the pack against the red-painted tabletop three times. She used to wonder why three—not two or four or even six, always three—tap, tap, tap. She didn't want to interrupt the mystery by asking him. He was so compulsively mysterious anyway. She loved those gentle tappings, calling the two friends to their rendezvous with the past.

After savoring the approaching mystery for a few moments, he flicked his wrist, and magically two cigarettes popped out of that sacred pack of pleasure. Then he nodded to DeeDee's direction as he offered her one.

She always said, "I really shouldn't," before smiling wickedly. She reached over to pick out a cigarette and carefully laid it on her napkin.

A long look of pleasure smoothed out Dodo's face. He winked. "Here's looking at *you*, kid."

Then they both gazed at each other with the excitement of long-distance hitchhikers who had just landed a ride all the way to San Francisco.

Everything was set; DeeDee, as usual, took the first step into the past. "Do you remember how much everything seemed to matter back then?"

By this time, Dodo already had an unlit cigarette hanging from the side of his mouth, dangling at a wobbly angle. The cigarette bobbing, his eyes were already looking out into the distance over thousands of miles of highway. He fiddled with the book of matches in a prolonged foreplay to delight, eyes narrowing, wringing out this moment as thoroughly as possible.

"Oh really, Dodo, what lovely trips we had." Her head trembled for a second, just long enough to set that graying red hair of hers aquiver. "Oh really, Dodo."

That was his cue. Very carefully he opened the sacred packet of matches. How amazing to think that fire could come out of those funny little cardboard sticks; a quick flick, and he offered the flame to her.

She loved the way the little fingers of his hand would open up like a fan as he gallantly waited for her to pick up, puff, and light her cigarette. Then almost daring the flame to burn his fingers, he brought it up to his own dangling cigarette and took an endless puff. He seemed to suck up all the pleasures of life on one side of his mouth and blow out all the frustrations from the other side, leaving him in a cloud of contentment. Then he shook his head as if he was seeing some fleeting truth that was transforming his life at this very second. There they were, Dodo and DeeDee, the dynamic duo ready to take on a whole continent.

After a sip of coffee and a few minutes of secondhand smoke, he stared at her, his face relaxed, his eyes blurred in some sort of psychedelic flashback.

She smiled and nodded protectively, perhaps a little sadly, then they set off in reverie quietly together.

They meandered among the memories while four young men played poker at a table to one side of them, and an elderly woman softly sang to herself at the table on the other side.

After several hands of poker and what seemed like countless repetitions of that lullaby, Dodo once again tapped the pack of cigarettes on the table, this time twice, to signal an ending.

To DeeDee, now those taps sounded like irritating mechanical jabs, reminders of that strangely, maddeningly ordered world around her, so alien to the idiosyncratic delicacy of her life. As always, she looked at him, hoping to see that this time, the signal had no meaning. He kept staring down into the depths of his empty cup. To no one in particular, he said, "Time flies when you're having fun." He had a maddeningly cheerful tone to his voice. Worst of all, his eyes were in focus.

Then he uneasily glanced around the room, slipping his pack of cigarettes back into his pocket before peering a little too casually at his watch. Dodo, well on the way to metamorphosing back into

Dwayne, turned to DeeDee with the opaque, reassuring look that therapists give their clients, that your-hour-is-up smile. "Guess I better be going home. Thomas will be wondering where I am. Oh, by the way, Frannie, are you seeing anyone now?"

She looked up slightly dazed at the figure, already rising across from the table, towering benignly above her, and took a big gasp of smoke-laden air. She patched up her disappointment with that much used wide-eyed charm of hers that she hoped would cover over any uncomfortable situation. With a dramatic good-natured flurry, she rose to the occasion, swirling up in her long faded flowered skirt to stand at his side. Her arm reached out, and the hand on her thin wrist made a curving motion like a flower wilting on its stem. "Why, I can hardly keep the gentleman callers from stomping all over my marigolds." She batted her eyelids and gave her shoulders a coy shake.

"As bad as all that?"

She smiled, put her hands on her hips, and tried to look as arch as she could. "Who said anything about bad? I still shave my legs at least in summer. I take my birth control pills religiously whether I need to or not, and I try to be nice to old people. Using the tools of your trade on me, my dear? If I had extra money, I would get my hair fixed before my head."

Dwayne's head was cocked to the side now; his lips were smashed together as if he was watching a deer but incorrigible child. "Far be it from me to interfere."

They both stood motionless by that table for a moment "Well, if you have to know, Sam was the last man who darkened my doorstep."

"Sam, which one was Sam?" For just an instant, Dwayne looked interested enough to forget about Thomas.

"Sam, Wrong Number Sam. The guy who called up one night for Dolores. By the magic of chance and dyslexia, he called my number."

"Maybe he was letting his fingers do the walking."

"The only walking he did was out my door, fingers and all."

"Off with his head, my red queen!" Dwayne's hand cut through the smoky air.

They were out the door now; even this part of town with dusty liquor stores and even dustier-looking old men were powdered with the gold of a summer evening.

"Oh, by the way, Frannie, Thomas mentioned that his senior partner seems to be interested in meeting a single woman. Imagine talking to Thomas about that!" Dwayne paused for a few moments. "He asked me what *you* were doing lately."

"Why, darling, my dance card is ever so full…maybe next year."

"Where's the woman who dared to trek across the country armed only with her thumb?"

Perhaps it was the gold rubbing off the buildings around her, or simply that she was a creature of hope; she began teetering in her resolve. "What if he doesn't want a woman of a slightly older vintage? You know how men are, looking for someone half their age and even then that's too old." She paused for a few discreet maybe even coy moments. "What is he like?"

"His name is Leonard. Leonard Grimbaugh."

"That doesn't sound promising."

"He's the person who hired Thomas a while back. I've met him a few times. He's okay looking, not my type at all. There's something tortured about him that you'll love. Come on, what do you have to lose?"

"To lose…" She paused and noticed the dusty sleeping man lying on the doorway of the restaurant they were passing.

Dwayne was too busy looking at Frannie with boundless sympathy to notice their new companion.

Not that she absolutely minded sympathy, but after all, there were so many people who really needed it more than her. At least that's what she hoped. "Well, I suppose so, just for you. But I will not go out on a date with him. If you want to bring him along to my July fete, I won't stop you." She put her chin up, and for a minute, ignoring her companions, she resurrected her allure and began parading regally through that shabby neighborhood.

Dwayne followed her like some prime minister. The dusty man in the doorway didn't notice anything at all.

CHAPTER 3

FOR SOME REASON, Frannie never felt particularly comforted after seeing Dwayne, though comfort was a commodity that seemed almost as rare as gentleman callers.

Her thin form, even at rest, pulsed with some sort of electrical charge that seemed to arouse people's interest but seldom attracted their touch and let alone comfort. Her heightened state of anticipation seemed to place her in a dimension slightly beyond the reach of companionship.

After she waved goodbye to Dwayne's car, she plunged once again into that urgent whimsy that she called cleaning; the fete was in nine more days. She could already hear the excited voices around her. "Frannie, you look fantastic as usual" or "Why, Frannie, you never cease to amaze me." She would hear her name spoken by laughing guests huddled in little groups. "You know, Frannie." How she loved to hear her name in almost any context.

And this year, she had something even more breathtaking to look forward to: a gentleman caller. Not that she would admit that to Dwayne.

In the last several years, she had begun cutting her losses when it came to men. Although truth be told, even at the height of her youthful appeal, men always seemed to escape her grasp. She was the one they dated just before they met someone who they wanted to marry.

The newly married couple always invited her to the christening of their first child, although she was never asked to be the godmother. She was, as everybody knew, a good sport but, well, a little too much.

True to the promise of her breathless hopes, with hardly a mundane intrusion, she woke up on the humid morning of her fete, smiling at the brilliance of this anticipated day. After all, she knew that her dreams had created this morning.

God couldn't have felt a greater sense of satisfaction when he looked out on the world on the seventh day and saw that it was good. She crawled out of her spongy bed, placed her feet on the clammy floor, and walked without a stitch of clothing on to the bathroom. She sat on the toilet seat; visions of her fete dancing in her head. Like some afterthought or even perhaps an embarrassing mistake, the lower half of her body released an object into the toilet. *Plump*! the sound startled her as if its origins were from someone else's body.

As if in answer to that strange voice in the toilet bowl, she said, "Oh my!" Her eyebrows raised in alarm. All the while, her head craned, stretching the parchment skin of her neck as if she dreaded a further reply from those nether regions.

Her usual spell of excited distraction seemed momentarily broken by that racket beneath her, leaving her disturbingly vulnerable to the vulgar worries of most humans. As the throne underneath her warmed, she became dangerously introspective and, for a few heartbeats, wondered how she could ever allow a man into her private and not altogether appetizing rites; men are so finicky when it comes to things like that. Oh my! Better to think about more pleasant prospects.

She had a remarkable capacity of erasing not only unspeakable physical intrusions but also those even more disturbing moments of self-awareness.

Sitting on that throne, she shook her head with something like determination and once again submerged herself in her multicolored dreams. Presto, she found herself in the shower, steamy water rushing against her dry skin and wiping away any apprehensions about the intrusive world inside or out.

Once again, her mind was left free to anticipate her magical afternoon. How she loved a hot shower on even the hottest of days. What an absolutely wonderful way to start to this marvelous, longed-for day. Absolutely, everything was perfect.

When she finished her ablutions, she toweled herself off and dowsed herself extravagantly with baby powder. She found herself enveloped in that perfumed cloud of mystery until a spell of coughing forced her to abandon the bathroom, leaving footsteps on the powdery floor. What a wonderful morning and not a minute to waste.

She stepped into the bedroom and accidentally glanced at her vanity mirror. She caught a glimpse of a naked form, pink and drooping, a plucked chicken of a naked form embarrassingly bereft of plumage. She jerked her gaze away from that strange image as if it was not her own. With a lifetime of discipline, she quickly turned away from that disturbing sight to the more pleasing pile of purple that comprised her fete costume. Laid out on the bureau, it awaited her like a suitor.

It was one of those hot and humid mornings in Minnesota that seemed like an implausible fantasy after the endless months of winter cold. In fact, it was so hot and humid that the wide brim of her fantastic hat had begun to droop over the side of the bureau. She was too busy slipping on underwear over her powdery body to notice.

Within minutes, she was more than presentable, most definitely robed in splendor. With hardly any apprehension, she looked in the mirror. If she blurred her vision just a little, she was almost the woman that she imagined she was.

The world outside that charmed bedroom was moving in underwater slow motion. At 9:00 a.m., it was already so warm that a neighbor's dog was digging a hole in the shade of Frannie's neglected garden, anything to find the relief of coolness. It was one of those very quiet Sunday mornings in which people hardly have the energy to make coffee let alone go to church.

The whole world was saturated and sluggish except for Frannie; she was incandescent. After all, she lived in a world separate from the rest of mortals, a place where things like weather never interfered with her anticipation.

Why, the morning simply seemed to disappear.

At 1:00 p.m., her guests began arriving, people whom she had known for years. She glanced to make sure that the wine and bubbly water were all on the dining room table. The bottles were sweating with the promise of coolness inside, dampening the table-cloth underneath.

On a smaller table by the living room window, a small bronze lion was puffing smoky incense out its nostrils. The old-fashioned phonograph was piled high with records: First, the Beatles, then Bob Dylan, Marianne Faithfull, Melanie, and finally, Cat Stevens. She had been in love with Cat Stevens. Oh my!

To the tune of "Let It Be," she waltzed to the door to meet Jeanne and Simon.

Frannie had lived with Simon in a commune years ago, even sharing a bed with him until he met Jeanne.

Frannie gave them both an extravagant hug. "How wonderful to see you both. Why, you're my favorite couple on earth!" She didn't mention how impossibly dowdy she thought Jeanne was looking. Thank goodness, they didn't bring their daughter, Sunshine. She always needed to be the center of attention, not that Frannie didn't absolutely adore that child. Child? Why, she must be twenty years old by now.

And Ralphie came next, bringing that little frayed red book of the sayings of Chairman Mao. Besides, it was the only time of the year that he could wear his red headband. That famous headband of his used to barely restrain his long brown locks; now it served as a kind of equator for the round balled expanse of his head.

She forgot what exactly he was doing now except that he always had a new car. Not that she really cared for things like that. He was married too for a second time.

Frannie had met the very young bride at the Calhoun Beach Club. He never brought his new wife to the July soiree; it was an event for grown-ups. Imagine being all grown-up! Besides he never stayed long, even then most of the time, he was on his cell phone. It seemed he was a very important man to the world at large.

"Oh, Ralphie, how dear of you to bring your little red book. Planning to start a revolution?"

"Not unless I can depose you, Frannie."

"Oh, go eat cake, Ralphie dear. Where is your young bride… taking a little nap?"

He smirked at her. "Say, now that you mention it, you look like you could use a little rest yourself, not that you don't look as fantastic as usual."

"I never look as usual. You should know that by now."

Just then Rosemarie came in with a whole box of food. In her twenties, she had been outspoken about world hunger; she even joined some group that expected to wipe out hunger in 1986. Since people were still managing to starve to death in 1987, she switched the focus of her life and started a very chic vegetarian restaurant in Linden Hills that specialized in dishes with wild mushrooms. Though her food interests were much more specialized now, she still seemed unable to break the habit of bringing huge quantities of food to any engagement she attended.

Rosemarie was the very first person who Frannie knew who actually called herself a lesbian. Lesbian—it sounded so poetic, although Frannie didn't really want to imagine what lesbians actually do when they are being lesbians.

Of course, Frannie was very supportive when her dear friend came out of the closet. After all, no one should have to live in a closet even if it is a bedroom closet.

Rosemarie was stocky with short hair turning steely gray, and her friend Theresa, who always floated along beside her, looked like an elongated version of Anne Frank—big doomed eyes staring out.

"Why, Rosemarie, how wonderful to see you!" Frannie stared at the heavily laden box in Rosemarie's arms. "Are you spearheading some sort of food drive?"

"Frannie, you look…so purple. Let's just say the box and its contents are insurance. I've tasted your cooking before."

Just as Rosemarie and Theresa began unpacking the wild mushroom quiche, the wild mushroom cold pasta salad, and the wild mushroom custard tarts; who should arrive late as usual but Dwayne;

she should have known he would be late (next year she must try to remember *not* to have him bring hors d'oeuvres). How that boy still loved to make an entrance!

Out of his car, he stepped, all tie-dyed and not a bit remorseful. He was carrying his tray of hors d'oeuvres crinkling under plastic wrap. Out of the other door stepped a stranger, a rather heavyset man who was taking small quick steps. His determined-looking top-heavy torso seemed barely connected to his darting, rapidly moving feet. The buttons of his very crisp shirt seemed to barely restrain the mass of his body. That whole package of a man was decorated with a paisley tie whose tight knot appeared to serve not only a decorative purpose but also to restrain anything that might slip out unexpectedly. Frannie's level of intensity revved up; she knew that this must be Leonard.

"Making your entrance again, Dodo darling. You can take the boy out of Queens but not the queen out of the boy."

He handed her his tray. "A bit testy, Frannie? Is it that time of month again? You're still having those times of month, aren't you?"

"Oh really, darling? I'm like some fine wine. I become more intriguing with age."

"Do I smell the bouquet of vinegar?"

"Here, let me take your tray. I need to keep you fresh for Thomas. We all know how he likes fresh young things. Where is he, by the way? Busy with some little lawyer foolishness? He is so busy, isn't he?"

"I don't want to talk about it."

"Oh dear. As bad as all that?" He paused briefly and, for a moment, looked like he might actually want to talk about something.

That vague possibility dissipated; the two slipped into their customary sparring routine.

Dodo flashed a smile. "Look who I have for you!"

"My darling Dodo, I thought that this was supposed to be a discreet meeting."

"The only thing discreet about you is your real intentions. Besides, I didn't want to deprive Leonard of the drama. You are always at your dramatic best when put to the test."

19

"Are you that starved for drama, Dodo? Married life a bit somber? I must have a little tête-à-tête with Thomas. Why don't you two plan a vacation, a second honeymoon? Get him away from all those boring papers, and make him dance barefoot in the sand under a tropic moon!" She handed the tray to a stunned Leonard, clicking her fingers like castanets, and started swirling, setting the birds on her skirt to flight.

Dodo—and he was clearly Dodo now—laughed and put an imaginary rose between his teeth and began spinning around with DeeDee. The guests, used to this annual ritual, began clapping their hands in time. For a moment, everyone seemed so much younger— young enough to want to be part of a spectacle. Only Leonard, with his fragile burden, stood immobilized. His eyes fixed in awe at every delicate movement of Frannie's hands. She spun a web of romantic nostalgia with every click of her fingers and kick of her purple-clad feet.

Finally, Ralphie casually announced, "Frannie, you know Frannie. She does this every year." The magic bubble burst; the clapping ceased and left the guests impatient for their hors d'oeuvres.

Frannie, true to form, didn't seem to understand that the moment was over; she kept snapping and swirling frantically in the center of her familiars.

Dodo, now Dwayne, was more resigned to endings. He stopped dancing and looked away as if he was ready to pick up the check and leave. Although the way he held his teeth clenched, he may have still been biting on the imaginary rose. Only Leonard's eyes hungered for more.

Finally, with exaggerated gentility, Dwayne said, "Frannie, allow me to introduce Leonard."

She stopped in the middle of a turn, disoriented for a moment to see all those blank faces staring at her. A practiced wide-eyed smile covered her face, and she graciously stuck her thin hand out to Leonard.

Only then did she realize that he was precariously balancing his burden. "What an absolute dear you are to hold that heavy tray while we indulge in our little foolishness. You ought to be ashamed of yourself, Dwayne. You didn't tell me how positively gallant your friend is. Now take his tray so that we can be properly introduced."

She lifted her pale hand to Leonard, and without missing a beat, he gently grasped those slightly trembling fingers in his much larger hand. With something close to awe, his fleshy neck barely contained by the paisley tie, bent; his lips brushing against the fluttery burden that had alighted on his hand. "I'm charmed, truly charmed."

Her guests watched Leonard's gallant gesture and then smiled at each other as if this meeting had been planned.

They broke out in applause; Frannie treated them to one last dramatic twirl. They all knew that this was her hour, the time of the year for childish hopes and the collusions of nostalgia. Frannie was indeed the queen.

Ralphie's cellular phone rang. "Good deal...I'll make sure he pays up. No, I'm not busy...just this little thing that's about over... yeah, yeah, yeah...I know it's not over until the fat lady sings. See you in twenty minutes."

Everyone rushed toward the food except for Leonard; he was following Frannie, and though she didn't turn around, she knew that she was being watched, maybe even savored.

As other less familiar people began filtering into the party, all ready for a spectacle. Dodo nudged DeeDee. "My dear, you're positively brilliant this afternoon...if a bit far-fetched."

"Far-fetched, this is my life darling, my life."

"I know."

As people began grabbing for drinks and food, the Beatles finally stopped singing. A harmonica, guitar, and the voice of Bob Dylan scratched through the afternoon.

"I would not so all alone. Everybody must get stoned."

CHAPTER 4

LEONARD WOKE UP as usual at 4:00 a.m. that next Monday. Also, as usual, he woke up covered in a slick coating of sweat, his heart pounding in his ears, beating like some swishing sped-up clock.

Not as usual, a lovely secret filtered through the racket of his pounding heart, not his usual run-of-the-mill secret that involved hidden strategies to maneuver people into compliance, but a different kind of secret that seemed to nudge him—warm, pulsing, and radiating excitement by sheer proximity.

Leonard was in love. Not that he really had someone to whom he could tell the secret. Intelligent, resourceful, determined to some people, and even admirable; he had never been familiar.

This morning, he actually jumped out of his damp bed, threw on a familiar robe that never quite seemed to stay closed over his expanding body, and walked to the bathroom. Only his image in the mirror once again reminded him of the desperate contingencies that ruled his life; his face congealed into his usual reserve. With both of his hands, he made a small apologetic gesture to that image of himself in the mirror and began walking with those small mechanical steps of his out of the bathroom and down the stairs.

He was on his way to the morning reunion with his coffee maker. What a perfect relationship they had.

At four-thirty every morning, it silently and automatically switched on. By the time Leonard reached the kitchen, the coffee machine had faithfully made a hot pot of coffee—coffee made dependably to perfection. He poured himself some, then, cup in hand, walked to his study where he turned on his desk light, and positioned himself in front of a stack of papers.

His day world had been set in motion; memories of the night were muffled by his daytime plans. A warm cup of coffee in his hand, he stared over his glasses, leafing through meticulously organized strategies for protecting that kingdom that he called Grimbaugh and Associates. He looked up for an instant as if he was trying to remember something…Frannie. A boyish smile broke through his determined congealed reserve.

He stood up. His large body rose like a ship, finally catching a morning breeze, lurching, and clanging in impatient motion. With direction and even a journey ahead, he hooded his eyes slightly into an alert, wary vigilance. His body moved with a powerful momentum while his head perched, a slightly disjointed lookout high above, watching for whatever dangers might lurk ahead.

At forty-seven years of age on a morning in July, even if it was one of those excessively humid mornings always leaving some part of him damp, his course was marked. He took a cold shower—his usual morning ritual to staunch the flow of his more private self. Not that he really noticed the temperature of the water on his body. When most men his age and weight began slowing down with vague and ominous complaints, his body seemed immune to pain or discomfort.

When he stepped out of the shower, he smeared deodorant on his ginger-haired armpits. His body moved in a kind of stringent economy of motion, not clumsiness, that would appear too vulnerable but rather in a kind of mechanical motion—steady, maybe even inexorable, like a knight in armor.

This morning, though, he interrupted his body's routine motion and took one very unnecessary look at the intimate stranger in the mirror. He saw that stranger's lips move: "Frannie." What a beautiful name. What an exciting person, dancing in the charmed circle of her friends. They loved her, a queen frolicking with her court.

For a moment, those tight eyes of his relaxed as he relived that glorious moment when she placed the tray in his hands, and he became her champion ready to vanquish anyone who threatened her.

Leonard studied that knight in the mirror with some disapproval. He reached to his forehead to pull a hunk of hair down over his naked forehead. There, that was better; his visor was down. He sucked in his hairy stomach and thrust out his chest.

In lieu of a lance, he grabbed his trusty deodorant stick and raised it in an epic salute. There, that was better. Should he call her? What if…what if…no, he mustn't think about that. He would simply talk to Thomas. Subtly of course, no need for him to know too much.

Without too much notice, Thomas could ask Dwayne for that precious phone number. How unfortunate that he had to betray his intentions before his conquest was secure! Not that his determination would not prevail in the long run, but secrecy left him more leeway to maneuver.

He pulled another hunk of hair across his head for added protection; he would prevail in his quest; he was invincible. For a moment, he envisioned the birds that swirled around his lady as she danced, yes, his heart that was beating in a gentler rhythm.

As for Thomas, he would better not see this as an opportunity for advancement; and as for Dwayne, who could take a man seriously, spent all his time listening to other people's problems.

Leonard looked away from the mirror.

With measured intensity, he drove his discreet gray Lexis and finally parked at his very own parking space over, in which the name Mr. Leonard Grimbaugh was stenciled.

A tall shiny building that reflected the sky towered over him as he stepped out of his car. Sweat was already wilting that carefully pressed shirt. He pushed through the reflecting glass door with even more purpose than usual.

"Good morning, Mr. Grimbaugh," the receptionist spoke with just the correct amount of enthusiasm to convey both pleasure and deference. With crisply applied makeup and her pageboy haircut, she seemed like some guardian angel whose whole vocation in life was to watch over the concerns of Leonard.

"Good morning, Kim." Leonard nodded just enough so that she knew he was pleased with her. She was after all almost perfect, so necessary and yet so replaceable.

She understood that nod and spoke with reverent satisfaction, "Thomas asked me to tell him when you arrived. He said that he wants to talk with you about some engagement you had this weekend." Then despite some years of practice, her studied look of amiable deference turned into something suspiciously like a teasing smile.

For a moment, Leonard felt that he was simply an overweight man on a hot day, steaming with mammal smells. This would never due. His face began stiffening into an inanimate mask while his eyes seared through her.

Her fresh face wilted under the heat of those eyes. She looked down chastened and rightly so. How dare she engage in blatant familiarity.

Finally, after a protracted term of punishing silence, certainly long enough to discourage future indiscretions on her part, Leonard gave her a temporary reprieve. "Kim, please have the BroadQuest file ready for review."

She raised her contrite face and said, "Yes, Mr. Grimbaugh. Immediately, Mr. Grimbaugh."

He looked satisfied.

She was once again his awestruck maidservant.

As he walked into his office, with little machinelike steps, he realized that he would delay calling his very junior associate until late in the day. Though Leonard still longed for that precious phone number, he must shore up the breach in his assaulted privacy.

Finally, at 4:30 p.m., he dialed Thomas. "Thomas, this is Leonard."

"Hello, Leonard, I was wondering how Sunday went."

There was a long and significant silence over the phone.

Leonard's voice droned on but perhaps just a little too carefully enunciated. "Thomas, I have some concerns about a couple of the briefs that you wrote last week. Stop in and see me tomorrow."

"Yes, Le—Mr. Grimbaugh."

"Fine. By the way, I want to write a thank-you note to Dwayne's friend. What was her name? Yes, Frannie, wasn't it? Do you have her address and perhaps her phone number?"

There was a long pause, this time initiated on Thomas's end.

Leonard silently took his glasses off and wiped his glossy face.

"You know, Leonard, I have a very busy day tomorrow. Can we put off that meeting until Wednesday?"

"Wednesday. Wednesday will be fine. I was only going to give you a couple of pointers. The briefs were quite adequate."

"I just happen to have Frannie's phone number with me. Dwayne and she are so close. I'm glad to be of use to you."

Again, there was a long silent wait.

Excitement pounded, flushing through Leonard's head, distracting him from his strategies. In the suspense of that silence, he became terrified that Thomas would not have that number, and that he, Leonard, would have to wait a whole twenty-four hours before hearing Frannie's voice.

And Thomas was taking his time. Finally, "Here it is, Leonard. Do you have a pen handy?"

"Of course."

"897-7873…got it?"

"Sure." Leonard sounded almost friendly or maybe just relieved.

There followed another pause; this one was more serene. After all, they both had gotten what they wanted.

They hung up simultaneously.

That evening on the way home, Leonard celebrated his triumph at The Bloomington Eatery. He had a sirloin steak, rare; a salad with blue cheese dressing; a slightly overdone and powdery baked potato; two martinis; and hope.

Before he actually called Frannie that night, he shaved and showered and mixed himself another martini. Sitting on his bed, hair smoothed over his forehead, garbed in his bathrobe; he reached for the phone with forced composure. His fingers began trembling. For a brief moment, no longer set in frozen resolution, he looked like a boy on Christmas morning whose long wait had come to an end.

The phone rang four times. Just as his body was beginning to harden against the impact of disappointment, he heard a voice on the other end. "Hello."

"Hello, is this Frannie?"

"Yes, can I help you?"

"Frannie, this is Leonard."

"Leonard?"

"You know, Dwayne's friend, the person you met Sunday." His voice cracked.

She paused to let that information sink in.

Truth be told, Leonard had been rather a disappointment for her. She had pictured someone more dramatic looking and not quite so large. She never tolerated disappointment for long; she simply forgot whatever had let her down.

Yes, she had forgotten about Leonard.

"Oh, Leonard. I'm so glad you called. I forget names so easily but never a face. I do remember you very, very clearly. I am ever so thrilled that you called. You were quite the gallant. How are you?"

"Oh, I'm just fine." He paused for a moment as he realized how fine he really was. "I spoke with Dwayne's friend Thomas this afternoon. I hope that it is all right with you, but I asked him for your number. I wanted to thank you for your gracious hospitality Sunday."

"Why, Leonard, you are gallant! What a nice thought."

There was a long pause.

"I know that so many men must want your company...but I was wondering...if I could take you out for dinner some evening."

For a silent moment, she resurrected her image of him: the way he kept slicking his thinning hair across his forehead.

Usually men had a way of disappearing after she was disappointed; now here was Leonard, popping up again like some mushroom after a warm rain, a surprise really coming out of nowhere. Was it that Frannie loved the zany surprise of it all or that something about his cracking, beseeching voice touched her?

Now that big man was standing by a phone, talking to her, and wanting her badly. She could almost see him floundering, reaching out to her to her across time and space.

27

"Why, I would absolutely love to go out to dinner with you, Leonard. What a lovely surprise." And she meant it.

"You would actually go out with me?"

"Of course, I would, Leonard. I am at your command."

"How about Friday evening?"

"Perfect."

Perhaps it was the word *perfect* Leonard was in charge again. His voice sounded deeper and more controlled. "I will come by Friday at seven p.m."

"Why, I can't hardly wait."

"I'll see you then." He hung up.

Frannie was left holding the phone against her ear, the sound of his plea still echoing.

CHAPTER 5

SHE PRIDED HERSELF on never giving up on anyone; of course, forgetting was another matter.

How she hated to abandon people. She hoped that her fetes were like some huge net gathering in all the people who may have wondered from her attention.

Truth be told, she needed some motivation other than sheer pleasure to bring her in contact with people. They never seemed quite able to live up to her expectations. Though her body brimmed over with the energy of plans for things to come, her eyes, when she wasn't actually trying to charm a person, had a curiously sad look—a look that expressed the subtle complaint that she deserved more from the people who needed her.

And, oh, how she was needed at her job—her job at the Veterans Home. Four days a week, she had the opportunity to brighten up the lives of men whose lives needed brightening.

True, being part-time activities director wasn't a well-paying job, but she had a chance to do what she did best: entertaining the troops.

Fifteen years ago, when most of her friends were getting married or at least settling down to some kind of a career that could help them forget about turning thirty, she alone seemed left to carry the banner of an earlier carefree time. Though absolutely everyone said how young she looked with her wiry body all coiled in enthusiasm, she noticed sometime after her thirtieth year that people started

29

to begin saying her name differently. People used to say, "Frannie," with eye-popping enthusiasm as if a party was starting, and they were invited. Now people said her name in a lower register, glancing back and forth; and then invariably they would follow up her name with "You know, Frannie" as if "Frannie…'You Know Frannie'" was her full name.

Even Dodo, who she had ushered back and forth across the country hitchhiking and who seemed to absolutely match her passion for men and romance, started graduate school in psychology and, even worse, began a permanent relationship with the very somber and ambitious Thomas. Dwayne, alias Dodo, began dressing in ties and sports jackets. Imagine that!

That's when Frannie decided that she should slip into some quasi-permanent job. She didn't use the word *career*. In fact, she saw her job as a heightened hobby, her *thing*.

After all, she didn't want to be too preoccupied with a silly career and miss whatever amazing thing that was bound to come her way some day. She began working at the Veterans Home.

During that protracted interval on which she was waiting for some amazing thing to happen, she worked her way through a series of doomed boyfriends. None of them actually died, although they all seemed to leave the relationship severely wounded. Perhaps she simply found them that way. But leave they always did, straying out of her life.

She loved to talk to Dwayne after their inevitable departure. "You know Vince. He was such a sweet man really. The fact that he is in and out of prison and can't hold a job down, I really didn't hold that against him. Such a sweet, wild darling. I miss him so."

As she aged, the intervals between men became longer and longer and even longer. Fortunately, her job satisfied some of her needs to care for those dear but troubled members of the opposite sex.

The Monday following her ever-eventful fetes, she sat playing the piano in her bright corner of the recreation room at the Veterans Home. It was oldie but goodie hour. She heard a rumbling voice coming out of a shadowy corner of the room. "Frannie, play *always*. Frannie, *always*."

Most of the men in the darkened corners were listening slack face to a football game on the television set hoisted high up on the wall. But it was oldie but goodie hour in the bright light of Frannie's corner. Though an overhead fluorescent light flickered dimly, she stationed two lamps on either side of the piano to chase away lingering shadows.

Old men barely shaven and young men unshaven and in wheelchairs began congregating around the spectacle of her talent. That scene was so much more dramatic than the rest of their routine shuffling lives, that circuit between bedroom, recreation room, dining room; and back again, days blurring into a routine of reluctant waiting.

And into that circuit entered Frannie dressed in diaphanous purple and smiling with reddened lips.

> I'll be loving you always,
> With a heart that's true always,
> When you're in a jam,
> Need a helping hand,
> I'll be by your side,
> *Always.*

Her reedy voice trembled and cracked under the strain of all that poignancy. When her red lips had finally released the last bit of wavering tenderness, her frizzed head tilted toward the ceiling in some desperate hope. Even with her not-so-subtle makeup, barely covering her weathered skin, she was a picture to behold.

The last plaintive echo disappeared into the droning of the football game on the other side of the room; each one of the men who took time to listen knew that Frannie was singing to him.

Then she winked at the closest man and said, "Come on, sing along with me. Don't be shy. Imagine that you're twenty years old, and you're out with your sweetheart. The sun is shining, and you feel glad to be alive…imagine! Don't let me do this all by myself." As her hands began pounding out the melody, her lips again began forming the magic words of that signature song of hers.

A kind of deep rumbling moan coming from every corner of that room joined in. "I'll be loving you always."

She returned home that afternoon.

July is such a deceptive month in the north. The temperature is warm, and the sky is summer blue; all around is green—an indelible permanent green that seems here to stay.

All the while, each day is a little shorter than the next. Night is edging in sooner and winter closer, and all the time, people think summer is just beginning.

The very first thing that Frannie did when she got home was to call Dodo. "Dodo, you wouldn't believe who called me up last night."

"Really?"

"Your friend Leonard."

"I'm not sure I want credit for that. He's not really my friend. He's Grimbaugh and Associates, and Thomas is an associate. I really only met him once before. Thomas won't admit it of course, but I think that Leonard is his hero—all grim and determined and single-minded."

"You married him, my dear."

"Eat your heart out."

"I'm a vegetarian. By the way, how did Thomas know that it would turn out this way?"

"Thomas may not know much about feelings, especially mine."

"Oh dear, what has that man done now?"

"Nothing special, just the usual. He never really listens. No matter what I say, he looks at me as if it is just another problem that he, busy man that he is, has to solve. Even worse, he actually tries to solve it. You know, men."

"Not lately I have to admit. For the last few years, I've been gradually becoming the amazing invisible woman even when I snap my castanets."

"You better watch out, DeeDee. You're starting to sound like one of those limp, slightly nuts heroines out of a Tennessee Williams play."

"Darling, there was a time when we both relied on the kindness of strangers."

"Yeah, but I found a career."

"And Thomas isn't a stranger?"

"How did we get into this again?"

"Back to Leonard, can't I call him by something a little more intimate like Lenny are Leo?"

"Or Nard?"

"What is his last name again?"

"Grimbaugh of course…Grimbaugh and Associates."

"Oh dear, a robber baron.

"Your very own."

"Why doesn't that sound reassuring?"

"What do you have to lose?"

"You flatter me."

"Oh, DeeDee, I didn't mean it exactly like that, but you're well past forty, and that job of yours hardly keeps you in castanets any more. If you were a client of mine, I would be scratching my head and suggesting that perhaps you have some unresolved intimacy issues."

"Spare me. I am a woman of independent means."

"Be serious now. Thomas says that good old Leonard doesn't have anyone in his life. He's got that big old house of his that he rattles around in."

"He does look rather soulful."

"That's the spirit. He's kind of a diamond in the rough. I know how much you like rough."

"Are you sure you're not thinking of yourself, darling?"

"So when are you going out with him?"

"He really was sweet, Dodo. He called me up. His voice was just crackling with nervousness. How I love sensitive men. For a while, I thought they were as extinct as the passenger pigeon."

"I can't imagine Leonard flying."

"No need to be catty, my dear. He was so brave. He really was. I felt like royalty. And then as soon as I said yes, he suddenly got all sure of himself and masterful sounding. I think he really likes me, Dodo. I think he does."

"I think he does."

That next afternoon at the Veterans Home, when she was finishing her oldie but goodie hour yet again with the plaintive strains of "I'll Be Loving You Always," her voice trembled more than usual as Leonard's face flashed across her mind.

When she got home, she was in the mood for mystery; she decided to take a bath instead of a shower. She turned the hot water faucet on; it coughed a bit and then started chugging out hot water. As the bathroom mirror steamed up, she walked into the bedroom, put on a record of the Moody Blues, and peeled off her clothes.

Snapping her castanets, she returned to the bathroom and there poured May Lilac bath salts into the splashing water. The mirror completely hazed over; she danced naked and dreamed of what could be: Leonard...what a dear man and so powerful!

When the tub finally filled with the white suds of May and she was beginning to become out of breath, she turned off the taps and slowly inched into that water that burned with comfort. Her whole body eased up and reclined back into the suds; she released a luxurious sigh. As she settled in, that disappointed look in her eyes disappeared amidst all the comforts. Only when the water began cooling to lukewarm was she once again set in motion. She began shaving her legs.

Even at the height of the long-haired au naturel sixties, she performed that rite of mutilation. Her grasp on femininity was tenuous enough without men actually seeing red hair curling up her legs. Her mother once said that Frannie legs were hairy as an orangutan's. The razor nicked her leg and drew blood. Frannie's whole body shuddered in the tub. No, she mustn't think of that.

By the time, Leonard drove up (she had been watching for his car out the window) and pressed her doorbell; she was very casually and moistly tending her plants. Through the glass door, he would be able to see her wafting from plant to plant to the strains of Pachelbel's "Canon."

At the sound of the bell, she looked up with faint surprise very serenely but of course warmly; she floated over to answer its call. The door opened and the strains of Pachelbel soaked into the evening air and Leonard. The rose he clutched in his big hand trembled. His hair was plastered across his forehead, and though he stood there solidly, almost defiantly, his eyes glanced down in shy excitement. He didn't want her to see his eyes; they put people off so.

"Oh, Leonard, how lovely to see you!" She shone there in the doorway, eyes twinkling like a night in May on his downcast head coaxing, almost teasing his eyes to look up. She loved shy men.

His thinning scalp slowly tilted upward, and his eyes reflected Frannie's charm back into her own face. He lifted his right hand, which held the still trembling rose, and said, "My lady."

Her bracelets jangled as she curtsied and then allowed Leonard to place the rose in her hand.

They both chanced onto one of those perfect moments when all life's stories seem to come to a point of possibility, when stumbling blindly suddenly a happy ending appears in sight, perhaps even a reward.

Frannie rested in those eager, lonely eyes of Leonard; Leonard was dazzled by his lady. And time stood still, a mountaintop of a moment where the world spread out beneath them. Why it was perfect!

Frannie clasped that rose with uncharacteristic determination. A thorn pricking her finger broke the spell and set her in motion. "Here I am, keeping you standing outside. What kind of a hostess am I?" She didn't really wait for an answer. "Come in, you make yourself right at home now. Would you like some herbal iced tea before we go?"

Leonard suddenly realized that he was feeling crumpled in the heat. How dare he enter this miraculous abode. Why there was even iced herbal tea. His head dropped again as if he felt daunted by the challenge of stepping over the threshold of a new and wonderful life.

Ever so casually and warmly as if they were old friends, she touched his shoulder.

He looked up, and all thoughts of being crumpled and sweaty were banished by the utter brilliance of her wide-eyed smile. "Yes, Frannie, I would like some." How he loved to say her name.

She ushered him into to that abode of green plants and lilting music and summer evenings.

What a wonderful summer evening. He didn't even care that one drop of sweat was carelessly running down the side of his cheek like a tear.

She deposited him on the large billowing sofa that she had cornered Dwayne and Thomas into transporting from a garage sale ten blocks away. Only after she had graciously walked, almost waltzed into the kitchen, did Leonard begin his usual reconnoitering—eyes bouncing from antique shawls laid over furniture to an old Kewpie doll propped up against the cracked mirror and a whole collection of glass balls each one filled with liquid, and inside the watery balls were different scenes from different seasons. Because of the heat, he was tempted to shake the ball with the snow-covered house in it, but somehow he felt that changing anything here would be a kind of sacrilege. This place was perfect; it was so true, just like Frannie.

Back in the kitchen, Frannie was taking as much time as possible to pour the tea. She took more care than usual picking out two glasses and actually wondered why nothing in her cupboard seemed to match. She found herself watching the drip coming out of her kitchen faucet and tried to discern some sort of rhythm.

There was a man in her house, a substantial, maybe even a determined man who wanted to be with her. How wonderful, how strange, how frightening. She just didn't want to ruin everything, you know, Frannie.

To buy herself more time, she said loud enough to be heard in the next room, "I was so pleased that you called. I really was. What a wonderful surprise!"

The sound of the refrigerator opening and closing, the gurgling sound of liquid being poured into glasses, a pause, and then the refrigerator door again, why, to Leonard, it was as beautiful and balanced as the strains of Pachelbel. In fact, all those sounds merged into the very essence of her.

He dared to add his own voice to that harmony. "Thank you, Frannie. It's my pleasure."

The disharmony of his own voice startled him. He quickly reached up to his head to make sure that a lock of his hair remained positioned over his forehead. Yes, all's well; he relaxed on the sofa to the sounds of her bracelets tinkling like temple bells.

She stepped out into the living room with a tray in hand. On it were two mismatched glasses and two saucers on which there were two brown knobby, sticky-looking objects. Frannie was on stage. "Peppermint tea, don't you just love peppermint tea on a warm evening?"

Leonard felt one drop of sweat coalesce in his armpit and drip down his side. "Oh yes, it's so refreshing."

"And those brown things are trail cookies. Dodo, I mean, Dwayne and I used to pack dozens of them when we went hitchhiking. I just mix together raisins and coconut and sunflower seed and then bind it with peanut butter and honey, and there you have it!"

"It sounds very nutritious." Leonard paused and didn't know what to say next.

"How sweet of you to notice."

CHAPTER 6

ONCE THEY ACTUALLY stepped into his car, they both knew that they were on surer ground; Leonard was driving. His hands gripped the wheel surely. His face stared straight ahead fixed on the distance except when his eyes fiercely shot back and forth across the night. And Frannie found herself settling into that soft seat next to her man.

The engine of that expensive car throbbed under her; its direction, sure.

Now they didn't need to speak; their silence was a contract. Peppermint tea to refresh them, trail cookies to give them energy, they set out on their journey together.

Almost as an afterthought, Leonard mentioned, "We're going to the Calhoun Beach Club. I've reserved a table for us. I hope that pleases you."

"Oh yes, it sounds so wonderful, Leonard." She was learning to say his name too. "Leonard, Leonard, Leonard."

She could see Lake Calhoun on her right as cars with their lights splayed out sped by. On her left, joggers and lovers were moving in and out of the shadows around the circuit of the lake.

Leonard drove into the parking lot. For a brief moment, in the silence with the dark profile of Leonard next to her, she wondered how this all could be happening to her. Then he took charge, turning toward her and smiling. The yellow light of the parking lot burnished his face. "You have no idea how nervous I felt about calling you."

"I had no idea…you looked so, so masterful." She lied, a white lie of course.

He smiled in the dim light of the parking lot, either pleased with the freedom of disclosure or at the effectiveness of his camouflage. "I want to show you off to the world tonight."

And he did. Everyone at the club seemed eager to greet him. "Hello, Mr. Grimbaugh," said the smiling young receptionist.

"Hello, Dianne, I'd like you to meet my special friend, Frannie."

"What a handsome couple you make."

The charmed pair walked up the broad staircase. Frannie touched the cool marble of the banister and turned to smile at Leonard. He didn't notice. He appeared to be walking just a step ahead of her as if he was a vanguard protecting her from this evening.

They reached the brightly lit summit and turned left in the high-ceilinged hallway.

"Why, what a wonderful chandelier! I feel like I am a princess at a ball."

He paused ever so slightly so that they were in stride again. His hand tightened around her arm. "You're my princess tonight, Frannie."

And then she heard the violin music in the restaurant.

"Good evening, Mr. Grimbaugh," said the maître d' in a solemn but ever so friendly tone.

Leonard subtly glanced sideways to see if Frannie noticed.

She did.

"Good evening, Rudolph. I hope you have something very special for us tonight."

"So pleased that you could come this evening, sir, and with such a lovely guest. We have succulent fresh lobster in a lime, saffron, and vodka sauce…superb tonight."

Rudolph led them through that starry Caribbean night of the dining room.

Tall palm trees arched and tables twinkled with candles and the music, the beautiful sad night music, engulfed them. All around people were eating quietly, each couple on an island with their private star.

Frannie could barely restrain herself from twirling and snapping her castanets. The maître d' gallantly but severely pulled a chair out of the darkness and motioned her to sit on it. She gave him a dazzling smile, and with just the hint of a spin, she sat down.

Leonard, substantial and secure, sat opposite her.

"Someone will be right with you." Rudolph showered an ingratiating smile on Leonard and departed to get ready for the next honored guests.

In the dim evening, all the guests seemed to be positioned at such discreet twinkling distances from each other—Frannie from Leonard and Frannie and Leonard from all the other guests. Only the tuxedoed staff seemed to provide moments of connection.

For a second, Frannie wondered if this was what it was like to be an adult—such a quiet, discreet, and safe distance. Even the crimson roses on the table seemed to stand sentry in front of her. "Oh, Leonard, this is wonderful!"

She looked at him over the flowers and across the wavering candle to see his face no longer quietly formal but actually icy staring across the room. His eyes seemed to catch the flame of the burning candle. For a moment, she thought that she had done something wrong and gave him her most innocent wide-eyed smile; she cocked her head in sympathy.

He glanced at her. "I told them that I wanted a table by the terrace. This will never do." Then he steadied his eyes on her and softened a little. "I wanted this night to be perfect for you."

"Why, Leonard, aren't you sweet! This is positively wonderful, a story come true." She tried to hold his eyes in the glimmer of the candlelight.

His head jerked toward another formally dressed person coming out of the shadow. A tuxedoed but pregnant-looking waitress approached and began hovering like a moth around the candlelit table and Leonard.

"Mr. Grimbaugh, would you and your guest like a drink before dinner?"

"This will never do."

The waitress tried to smile.

"When I made this reservation, I told them that I wanted a table by the terrace."

For a moment, the starched smile of the waitresses crumbled. Then she quickly smoothed out her face. "Mr. Grimbaugh, I am so sorry for the inconvenience. Let me talk with the maître d'."

He gave her a sharp nod.

The maître d' appeared. His crisp formality now transformed into deep apology. "There must have been some sort of a mistake, Mr. Grimbaugh. I'm sure it is our mistake. I am deeply sorry that we have inconvenienced you."

Leonard nodded coldly.

The maître d' knew that his job wasn't finished yet. "You are our guest here. This"—he motioned subtly and reproachfully toward the waitress—"won't happen again. The table by the terrace is being cleared as we speak. Can I offer you a drink now, and then I will escort you and your lovely lady to the other table?" He smiled at Frannie.

She had been sitting rather stunned, listening to the altercation. "Oh, Leonard, I'm fine here. This is so wonderful."

Leonard shot a quick silencing look at her and then turned his reproachful stare back at the maître d'.

"Of course, Mr. Grimbaugh, due to the inexcusable inconvenience, the dinner this evening will be the club's treat." He smiled down soothingly at the two guests.

Leonard answered with a cool, vanquishing smile. "My dear, what would you like a drink?"

Frannie knew it was her turn to speak. She thought for a moment. Then her face conspicuously lit up, the way it did at the Veterans Home. "You know, I think I'll have a gin and tonic. What's a summer evening without a gin and tonic?" She showered her good will on both the maître d' and her champion.

Leonard really was her champion, wasn't he? A diamond in the rough…perhaps a little cutting but so precious.

"I'll have a martini straight-up."

A very composed maître d' nodded to Leonard, and then he gallantly bowed to Frannie.

She simply said, "Oh my."

41

CHAPTER 7

THE BED STIRRED as she woke that next morning. She opened her eyes to a gray sullen day. Her nose was cold. When she sniffed the air, she could smell winter waiting in the wings.

Normally after her fetes, the threat of summer ebbing frightened her. She hated winter, getting up in the dark, catching a bus at the corner while shadowy huddled strangers puffed steam into the frigid air. She always felt alone and somehow abandoned.

Not that her clients at the Veterans Home would have known that. Even on the coldest day in January, she would spring into the hot antiseptic-smelling building, shed all the gruesome paraphernalia of winter in her tiny office, and head out into the recreation room to shower her men with good cheer.

"My, aren't you looking fine this morning, Herman!"

Herman would look up from a crouched position in his wheelchair, wondering why someone was saying his name so early in the morning. When Frannie touched his stubbly cheek, he would shake his head gruffly with the hint of a smile.

She would move on. "What a lovely plaid shirt that is Leo, so festive."

Leo would look down on his shirt between bites of breakfast and brush off an errant cornflakes.

Truth be told, they were all a bit protective of this preposterous gal who fluttered in each morning. They watched her change during the ten years that she worked there from a young woman acting outrageously to an older woman who tried outrageously to be young. Like many fair-skinned people, her dewy peaches and cream complexion seemed over the years to be gradually transformed into finely wrinkled parchment. Thanks to cosmetics and a rather heightened personality, she was still just as colorful.

She sat up in bed, the bedsprings singing, "Yes...last night... Leonard." Her eyes widened; a childlike smile warmed her face.

That night, there was another more definite call from Leonard. This time, Frannie was more than benevolent; she was ready, her head filled with imaginings of glamorous evenings, her stomach filled with warm gravy of being loved. It was like setting off hitchhiking across country with Dodo, except Leonard was so much more protective and she...so much more desirable. Both of them held their phone receivers basking in the inevitability of it all.

Frannie invited him to her house for a special dinner from an old cookbook of her deceased mother. Although normally she avoided cookbooks in favor of a more impressionistic and whimsical culinary style, she decided to try to outdo herself for her suitor.

She settled on a recipe for salmon loaf with a special lemon sauce, baked potatoes (What could possibly go wrong with baked potatoes?), and a salad that Dodo used to bring to potluck dinners: chopped-up lettuce; imitation bacon bits; crunched-up uncooked ramen noodles from an instant ramen noodle packet dressed with ketchup, a packet of onion soup mix, and Wesson oil. Though she had lived her entire life in Minnesota, she wanted to impress Leonard with the breadth of her culinary skills.

And indeed, Leonard was charmed with the flutter of her preparations, although he was perhaps a bit noncommittal about the meal. Perhaps his mind was on dessert.

She actually had a dessert planned though. Since he had appeared to enjoy those knobby brown balls of raisins, peanut butter, sunflower seeds, and honey, she served them again.

Leonard took one look at those concoctions. "How gracious of you to invite me. I can't eat another bite." He gently patted his stomach and suggested that they sit at the couch. "No, I don't want herbal tea."

"What a dear man you are," she said very fluttery. "Let me tidy the kitchen a little."

His head hung down like a boy who had just lost his puppy.

"Oh, I suppose I could leave things out." She winked at him benevolently and then giggled nervously like a little girl.

Leonard pushed his chair out, bowed to her, and motioned masterfully toward the sofa. Frannie composed herself and followed. He seated himself in the middle of the sofa. As if by habit, she sat nestling next to him. He put his arm around her, pulling her even closer. He breathed warm and excited on her cheek.

She smelled salmon and ketchup on his breath. He pressed his face to hers and stuck his warm moist tongue in her mouth. She would have said, "Oh my," if she could have but instead began accustoming herself to that soft damp probe in her mouth. Though she knew that this was an expression of matrimonial ardor, she found herself struggling, but she began thinking about being on the road again: blue sky and Dodo at her side, and then she let go. This was just another trip.

* * *

For the climactic third date, Leonard invited her to the sumptuous 510 Groveland restaurant and then afterward to his place.

In the car after dinner that evening, they sat solemnly, oncoming car lights momentarily illuminating their faces; they both knew what was coming next, her face almost as frozen as his. For reassurance, she touched his substantial leg. Yes, this was meant to be.

It was an unusually cool night at the end of July. The stars, no longer hazy with heat, burned more brightly.

As they stepped out of the car silently, they both looked up surprised to see the stars very close. Their footfalls echoed in the air. Frannie noticed how the crickets had already begun singing louder to mark the ending of summer.

This year, she hardly cared. She knew that she was under the protection of a man who seemed to control everything. His keys, jangling like glass breaking, opened the door.

"Come in, Frannie. I've been waiting for this moment for a lifetime."

"Oh my," she smiled and looked down while her pumping heart rushed blood to her head.

The sound drowned out the crickets. She stepped into the house and was immediately surrounded by illuminated fragile objet d'art placed throughout the living room for viewing. Even the stiff leather-covered furniture seemed more for sight than sitting.

Leonard had been collecting things ever since he bought his first antique as a freshman at Harvard's business school. In fact, when other students were parading around campus with red bands tied around their heads and picket signs in their hands, enjoying the picnic of student revolution, he was busy studying.

But each Saturday morning, he would leave his books and for two hours scour the upstate New York countryside for antiques.

His very first treasure was an extraordinary candlestick made of lead. On it, Huckleberry Finn rubbed clean of paint was holding a slightly drooping fishing pole as he leaned against the candleholder. There was a dog of some indeterminate breed loyally sitting at Huck's feet. For the first few months, how Leonard prized that possession like a memory of some carefree childhood that had never been.

By graduation, he had collected many and more expensive antiques, and that candlestick wistfully was laid aside. Though he definitely didn't want that clumsy thing on display, he felt a certain need to have it somewhere in his possession.

At the oddest moments, he would find himself remembering that old thing and always felt compelled to search through his unwanted possessions tidily stored in a large rather dark closet, just to be sure that that funny thing was still there.

After much too much effort, he would finally come upon it, only to be once again reassured that it wasn't really up to the rest of his collection, not at all.

"Please sit down, my love." His face was frozen into what he thought was a cavalier smile. Only his hands betrayed his nervousness. "Would you like a drink?"

"That would be nice. What a beautiful home you have...so many lovely things." She sat down a little gingerly. She was impressed, all those shiny, fragile objects crowding in around her. For her own tastes, though, she avoided things that could shatter so easily. Not only must they take days to dust, but also one impulsive swirl of her skirt (and she was prone to the sudden impulse to dance) could lay waste to the entire collection, leaving lethal shards of glass littering her floor just waiting to pierce and tear her naked feet. Yes, Leonard's things were beautiful in a slightly dangerous sort of way.

He walked into the dining room, abandoning her to the wonders of the sitting room. Normally as a master of efficiency, he would not have spent so much time away from his guest, but he needed time to relax, to steady his hands.

He returned to the room with delicate crystal glasses and a dark bottle of champagne positioned carefully on a silver tray.

She didn't have to wonder if the champagne were expensive, and though the cut glass caught the light, her body stiffened in an attempt to restrain any impulsive whirling motions.

He set his burden down on the cool marble table with sure mastery. His hands tamed now; he pulled the cork out of the bottle with a popping sound that not only released the pressure in the bottle but set the conjugal pair laughing hysterically.

For such a large man, Leonard had a high-pitched laugh as if his throat was so tight that only a kind of whistling sound could escape.

Frannie, for such a delicate woman, had a lower-pitched and ragged laugh punctuated by gasps.

Leonard achieved control first. After one particularly loud gasp, Frannie followed suite. They looked into each other's eyes in unspoken conspiracy.

Frannie had brought her toothbrush. Leonard had not only changed the sheets but also all the linens in the house.

"To us!" His eyes gleamed as brightly as his crystal glass.

"To love!" Frannie, used to adventures, was the first one to use that word.

They clinked the sparkling glasses together, and they both tasted the sharp pungency of that moment bubbling in their faces.

Relieved that the glasses hadn't shattered, she smiled. "What wonderful wine! It's like drinking angel tears."

He smiled, pleased with her whimsy. "I hope I'll never make you cry."

As if by some signal, they both placed their glasses on the table and reached for each other. In some well-practiced choreography, he took the lead and pulled her into his arms slowly pressing her even more deeply. Letting go into the substance of his determination, she tasted champagne and didn't know if it was her breath or his. Yes, this was it; this was finally it—a kiss to waken her from restless slumbers.

Afterward all she could remember of that night was the cool crisp sheets and that large form looming above her in the candlelight, naked and heavy, pushing into her with an insistence that she had never experienced before. She knew she was safe in the treasury of his heart.

CHAPTER 8

"OH, DODO, HE's wonderful. So sure of himself."

Dwayne seemed to catch the contagion of Frannie's excitement even across the telephone wires. "Did you do *it* last night, DeeDee, the big deed?"

"Let me simply say that I know that man, and that man is Leonard. I was beginning to think I would never feel that way again."

"Yeah, how many years do you have to go without sex before you can call yourself a virgin again?"

"I don't know, but it doesn't matter anymore."

"Since when were you that crazy about sex? I remember when we went hitchhiking, you always said that I was your boyfriend whenever a guy started to come on to you. For a while, I thought that you were in love with me."

"Heaven forbid."

"It wouldn't have been that bad."

"What would Thomas say?"

"I didn't know him back then, remember?"

"I guess I never think about you without Thomas anymore."

"Is it that bad?"

"Not bad exactly, but you never seem to be anywhere long without having to rush back into his arms or at least calling him, like you're afraid you'll turn into a pumpkin or something if you don't hear from him."

"You never did like Thomas."

"I don't want to talk about Thomas."

"So was he good? Was Leonard Grimbaugh good in bed? Thomas is dying to know."

"Why? Does Thomas want to take lessons or something? From what you say, he could use them. Sounds like he's a bit low on the ardor scale."

"Maybe it has something to do with being a lawyer."

"Excuses, excuses. Do you want me to rate Leonard on the lawyer or human scale?"

"Do I hear a note of sarcasm there, Frannie? Not a good sign after only the third date...the big date."

"Do I note some vague dissatisfaction with tea totaling Thomas, fastest man on the Internet?"

"Why do you always have to make such a big deal of things? I just wanted to know if you had a good time last night."

"I did. Promise you won't squeal about it to Thomas? Leonard is so discreet, you know."

"Cross my heart and hope to die."

"I'm serious, although laying down your life sounds a little severe."

"Okay."

They both hunkered down in their respective chairs. Frannie smiled deliciously.

"Well, he's a big man in more ways than one and even more determined than he looks, but still sometimes when we're all alone together, he seems like a little boy who just wanted to be loved."

"The great wounded rogue male...perfect."

"Does that mean he's got to die at the end?"

"You'd make an even better widow than a bride."

"What's that supposed to mean?"

"Never mind. I have to make supper for Thomas."

"See you next week at the Laughing Cup?"

"Would I miss your company and all that cigarette smoke?"

"I'm seeing Leonard again tonight. He seems so full of plans for us...trips. Very discreet and romantic."

"Maybe into the sunset?"
"As long as it's warm."

*   *   *

Frannie and Leonard settled into a routine that fall. Leonard would call her one night, then she would call him the next. He would take her out on Friday night after which they would tussle in his sheets.

They would spend Saturday morning drinking coffee and giggling in bed. On Saturday afternoon, they would go shopping, and Frannie would cook supper at her place.

Leonard began paying for the groceries and also suggesting the menus. They would usually drive back to his place Saturday night; Leonard thought that it was so much more comfortable than hers. She felt so pampered at his place that she hardly minded.

That year, she didn't have to struggle so desperately to make it through the frozen darkness of a Minnesota winter.

Leonard was very protective of her, chauffeuring her around all weekend. Occasionally he even picked her up at work when it was a particularly bitter day. He worried about her standing all alone at a bus stop; the snarling wind snapping at her, his darling.

And then it was Valentine's Day. He gave her dozens of roses and treated her to a weekend at a special suite of the Calhoun Beach Club. Oh my!

It was a Saturday evening in early March, the ground was still covered by a foot of snow; but on sunny days, water from the eroding snowdrifts ran along the sunny side of city streets.

Frannie was throwing together tuna casserole a la Frannie. (She thought that cooking with fish was sophisticated.) Leonard seemed absolutely distracted. While she mixed together cream of mushroom soup, tuna, noodles, and was adding her special ingredient, barbecued potato chips, she began wondering if possibly his fascination for her was on the wane.

Just as she had slid that culinary treat into the oven, he stirred from what seemed like apathy and broke the silence. "I have worked so hard in my life, Frannie. When I was a child, everyone thought

I was intelligent, brilliant. I was, but what no one realized was that I had to work hard. Just hard work isn't enough though. I needed a plan. My plan was to be lawyer—the best and most powerful lawyer around. When the other boys were running wild, I was inside studying. I had a plan. My parents weren't wealthy, so I knew I needed to get a scholarship to the best school around.

"When I got to Harvard on a full scholarship, I knew that if I was going to be the best, I needed to study even harder—so hard that no one would have a chance to beat me. When my classmates were wasting their time doing all the immature things that college students do, I had my plan.

"I graduated summa cum laude. When all the other lawyers were getting married, I had even more work to do. I needed to set up a company and then make that company work. Finally, that afternoon at your party, when I saw you and all your friends dancing and having fun, I knew that it was my turn now. And who would I share my pleasure with but you, the queen of the ball."

"Oh my." Frannie was at her most wide-eyed.

He continued with her absolute attention, "My company is one of the top firms in the Midwest. I've made it. I'm ready now. I want to go on a real adventure, not just an ordinary vacation.

"Ordinary people take vacations. That's not for us. You see, Frannie, I want you to come along, wandering through Italy, looking at all those wonderful museums, drinking fine wine, eating good food, and living the good life together. Would you come with me?"

She covered her face with her thin hands, hiding her pleasure and confusion. Finally, struggling for words, she looked up at her suitor. "I have always wanted to go to Italy. It's so warm and sunny and filled with romance. I used to love to read about Rome when I was child. So many wonderful and terrible things happened there. I'd love to go with you. Twenty years ago, Dodo and I—that's what I used to call Dwayne then—were going to go there, use Eurail passes and sleep in youth hostels, but then he fell in love with Thomas, and that was that." She halted and once again covered her face. "But, my dear, I simply don't have the money. I work part-time at the Veterans Home. I have to live very simply."

They sat there quietly, Frannie looking down, flustered while Leonard watched her, his face flickering—first, hard as a mask and then soft as a tender morning. Some inner dialogue, maybe even an argument, was taking place inside him. Finally, the softness prevailed.

"I really want you to come, Frannie. I have been thinking about this for a while. I didn't want to say anything right away. I can see that you live humbly, not that there's anything wrong with that. It's kind of exciting. You are gypsy, but we are getting older. You need someone like me. I know this may seem premature to you, but I've thought about this seriously."

He was looking at her with the softest eyes of anyone she had ever known. His substantial body, which had been sitting so inert, began to shift, and then he stood up. He reached into his pocket to pull out a small box. His hands were shaking. He opened that box and picked out a small object shining even brighter than his crystal glasses.

Frannie's head was still drooping, but she had begun gathering her wits. She watched him from the corner of her eye. It was like a dream, so slow and so inevitable.

He was on his knees in front of her now.

She lifted her head.

"My darling, Frannie, will you marry me?" As soon as he had actually gotten those words out, he looked stunned and frightened. He was so unused to needing someone else for his plans.

Her confusion faded; her face became still, not flustered, or even charming. A man of substance was proposing to her. Then she recognized his dear confusion and his longing. This man on his knees needed her as no one had needed her before. She placed her cool hands on his face.

Leonard lowered his head to her lap where she cradled him with a soft rocking motion.

She could feel his breath on her fingers, regular and gentle like of a sleeping child. They sat there lost in time. Only after the old refrigerator shuttered and began gently rattling, did she remember about the ring and the question. She lifted his face gently. He startled a bit as if she had actually woken him.

There on his face still lingered the peacefulness of sleep. She bent toward him so that their faces were inches apart. Searching deeply into his eyes, she said, "My dearest man, I would love to be your wife."

This was his cue to delicately lift the ring out of the box and slowly, so slowly, slip it on to her finger.

She felt the cool band sliding down her finger, Leonard's ring. She was his now.

There that was done; part of Leonard would always be around her now, taking care of her. It was so simple and easy that she wondered why this had never happened before.

* * *

Two days later, one of her teeth cracked while eating pasta at D'Amico's. *Oh my!*

Leonard looked over at her between bites of his risotto. In seconds, all contentment was wiped from his face. For an instant, he looked startled, even frightened, but almost immediately his face hardened into a vigilant stare—the face of a man on guard who had just heard a strange sound in the night. "Frannie, what's wrong?"

For an instant, she was shocked by the transformation, and then slowly it began sinking in that this was concern about her. How wonderful that someone could actually panic about her distress, like sympathetic labor pains. Even better, instead of being frightened by that nasty surprise inside her body, she could comfort him. "Oh, it's all right. I'm just fine. It's just that I think I cracked another tooth. Just one of the prices of middle age, you know. I'm fine, my love."

"Do you want to see someone tonight? Does it hurt? Do you have dental insurance?"

Frannie was actually forgetting about the catastrophe in her mouth in an effort to keep track of all the questions. "You are such a darling to be so concerned about me." She paused, collecting her thoughts. "No, I don't need to see anyone tonight, and it doesn't hurt nearly as much now that I know your here…and I don't have insurance."

"No dental insurance?"

"No dental insurance."

"Didn't you consider that you might need dental insurance just for this kind of situation?"

"Oh, I don't want to think about that now. I just don't."

"You just don't want to think about something that is so important?"

"I'll just call my dentist again. I'll find a way to pay for it. He is very understanding."

"Don't you think that it is about time you started paying attention to things instead of counting on strangers?"

For Frannie, this wasn't fun anymore. "He's not a stranger. He's had his hands in my mouth for twenty odd years."

"How understanding is he, Frannie? What do you have to do for him?"

"I'm sorry I ever mentioned it to you. I'll figure this out on my own."

"So when things get tough you threaten to leave me?"

"I wasn't threatening to leave you. I just don't want to be cross-examined anymore."

"I'm not cross-examining you. Is this the kind of gratitude that I can expect from you?" His face now looked like a stony mask. Only the eyes seemed animate, and they burned into Frannie.

"Please stop this, Leonard. I'm sorry I brought it up. I didn't mean to hurt you."

"Frannie, I'm trying to help you. Don't you see…and then you treat me this way."

"Oh, Leonard, I know it's because you love me that you care so deeply. Maybe I'm not used to someone loving me that way. I'm sorry. You are such a dear. I guess I wasn't myself. I was just a little upset about my tooth cracking."

His face seemed to be softening. His eyes still had a little of that scary fire in them, but Frannie began recognizing him again.

"The first thing tomorrow, I'll start looking into dental insurance for you. By the way, do you have health insurance?"

Frannie looked down and didn't answer.

He began looking cross again, but then some gentler emotion began to prevail. "What would you do without me? We'll get all these difficulties worked out. I want to be your husband, Frannie. I want you to count on me for everything."

She was close to tears; funny how she was close to tears. "Oh, Leonard, I do love you. You are so resourceful. What did I ever do without you?"

"You can always count on me. You need to understand that." There was hardly a note of complaint in his voice.

When they went back to Leonard's house, he made love to her with a fierce passion. She had a very slight headache. Fortunately, she didn't let that get in the way of his pleasure. She wanted him to know how grateful she was.

In the morning, he was full of plans for their honeymoon trip to Italy. The fairy-tale ending was materializing before Frannie's eyes.

A lifetime of hope was finally coming true. As far as that dull headache that still lingered, she had so many better things to think about. He was dear when he was excited…so much like a little boy. She could almost forget about that funny look on his face last night.

CHAPTER 9

INSTEAD OF FRANNIE'S usual July fete that year, an even grander event was going to be held at the Calhoun Beach Club to celebrate the nuptials of Leonard Grimbaugh and Frannie Fortunato. Though she had shared with Leonard her dream of the perfect wedding, two lovers in white tunics decked in flowers, reading Kahil Gibran to each other against a backdrop of tie-dyed sheets, flowered friends frolicking around them—a kind of nuptial Woodstock.

Leonard, who, of course, was charmed by the idea, decided that he would hire someone called an event organizer from the Bloomington offices of Celebration Inc. He didn't want to tax his bride-to-be.

Frannie was putting her house up for sale, and Leonard knew that she would be too busy to handle all the intricacies of the event. She really didn't mind, not really. Besides, they both knew that she had a way of forgetting things.

At the end of June, she gave up her part-time job in preparation for becoming a full-time wife.

That last Friday at the Veterans Home when she sang, "I'll be loving you…always," her eyes shone with tears, and her voice wavered even more poignantly as she drew out the last word of that last song—that final moment stretching out like some rubber band until it finally snapped, leaving her sitting there startled.

That afternoon, her men had even turned the television off. They gathered around her, and Herman handed her a card and a small messily wrapped parcel. She opened the card. On the front of it were pictures of colored balloons. On the inside it read "Bon Voyage."

Twenty names were untidily squeezed under that message. She opened the parcel. Inside was a wooden plaque with the word *always* burned into it. One of her men made it in the arts and crafts room. How she hated endings, especially when she was the one saying goodbye. She ran her fingers over that hallowed word and felt guilty.

That evening, Leonard began allowing his soon-to-be spouse the privilege of calling him Lenny, or in especially conjugal moments, "Dear Len." Though he still preferred her to call him by the more proper "Leonard" in public, he did seemed pleased that someone was close enough to him to use an endearing epithet.

The Thursday before the anticipated nuptials, DeeDee and Dodo were having a rather restrained stag or perhaps stagette party at the Cracked Cup. This was their monthly rendezvous after all.

In the gray haze of cigarette smoke, they began to go through their usual routine, with taps and long drawn on drags, but today at least the magic seemed to falter.

Up until these last few months, Frannie had led a rather single-minded existence. The focus of that single-minded life may have flitted from dream to dream weaving in and out of consensus reality, but she kept her focus on one imaginative panorama at a time. Since the advent of Leonard, she was beginning to pay the price for a dream of substance.

She couldn't forget about Leonard or consign him to a ritualized schedule. His rather large and prepossessing self-demanded almost constant attention. She was beginning to actually have to make choices, to choose between conflicting claims on her life...oh my!

Even Dodo seemed strangely discontented in that cloud of smoke that he had just exhaled. They found themselves shifting and straightening their chairs, gradually edging closer together until they were huddled, sharing each other's mammal warmth—the way they had once huddled during those cold days out on the road together, and waiting for a ride with their thumbs stuck out.

"Are you excited, DeeDee?"

"Yes, I suppose so, but sometimes I feel"—she shook her head in vague confusion—"like everything is kind of hazy around me."

Dodo looked into the smoky room. "It is, DeeDee."

"No, I don't mean that." She stared at him the way she used to when they found themselves stranded in the middle of nowhere, wondering if they would ever get another ride.

He frowned slightly. "There comes a time in everyone's life—"

"God, you sound like a therapist."

"It's an occupational hazard."

"I think I'm a little afraid."

"It's a big step."

"Now you tell me."

"What are friends for?"

"Are you and Thomas happy?"

"I suppose so."

"Why doesn't that sound convincing."

"I don't know."

"I wish you sounded like a therapist now. They know everything."

"I do?"

"You're supposed to, aren't you?"

"I've always been a rebel."

"Without a cause."

Dodo glanced from side to side cautiously. "Thomas and I don't talk much. I suppose that's not exactly true. We actually talk quite a bit. We talk about things, everything but about ourselves."

"I've spoiled you."

"Thanks for the sympathy."

"I suppose I got out of practice, giving you sympathy. Your life seems so perfect, a good job, a handsome husband. You always seem like you're living the good life. You don't need to look back. Now just as I have the chance to start my own good life, you tell me you don't know that it's all it's made out to be."

"You *have* gotten out of practice."

"Sorry."

"Thomas and I talk about a lot of things: what vacation we're planning, the whirlpool we're installing in the bathroom, even politics when I can stand to listen to him complain about taxes, but somehow if we talk about ourselves or at least if I talk about myself, he looks bored or even disappointed."

"Isn't he even interested in your dreams? Sometimes on our trips, I could hardly wait for morning to hear the next installment of the wacky wonderland you called sleep."

"I don't dream much anymore, or I suppose, to be more precise, I don't bother to remember them. I still remember the look on Thomas's face when I started telling him about the recurring carrot dream—how painful it was to be pulled from the soil."

"He didn't love that?"

"He's not into vegetables."

"Leonard is really good to me. I guess I am afraid. If things don't work out, well, what if finally, finally Leonard decides he's not into vegetables or doesn't like the sound of castanets? I know I shouldn't worry about that. He's so attentive. He even put my name as his next of kin on his will."

"You're not thinking of poisoning him, are you, DeeDee?"

"My cooking isn't that bad. It's just that I don't have a home anymore or even a job. Not that I was that great at setting up a life for myself, but I have no place to hide anymore."

"Is that bad?"

"I don't know."

"Are you happy with Leonard?"

"I suppose so."

"That's what I said when you asked me."

"Everything we talk about always turns into circles."

"It's okay, isn't it, DeeDee?"

"What?"

"Going in circles."

"I don't know. I guess it's all I've ever done."

"Think of it this way, DeeDee. If worse comes to worse, we still have Thursdays at the Cracked Cup, which reminds me, it *is* Thursday. I need to pick up some chicken breasts for Thomas's supper tonight. We have chicken breasts every Thursday. He's on a low-fat diet."

"I'm not sure Leonard likes my cooking."

"When has that stopped anybody from liking you?"

"Swell!"

"Good luck on Saturday. I'll be the first one to kiss the bride."

She frowned at him archly. "I'll think you'll be the second."

"Picky, picky, picky."

CHAPTER 10

A TUXEDOED CHAMBER quartet squeezed out strains of music as
the first two guests peered through the doorway and into the splendid ballroom of the Calhoun Beach Club. And even though rain
was pouring down outside and splattering against the windows, the
ballroom sparkled in manic brilliance.

As guests entered, they were also greeted by a huge mirror that
covered an entire wall. The mirror seemed to reassure the guests that
if the ensuing celebration were too brilliant, they could safely watch
this much anticipated event in reflection only.

A very discreet and buffed young woman from Celebrations
Inc. named Wanda was straightening bows on the myriad of white
bouquets that not only were spaced throughout the hall but also dramatically graced the steps of a huge narrow stairway that descended
from a rather mysterious-looking doorway on the second floor.

Leonard looked down from the summit of that grand stairway in guarded appraisal of the arrangement. The discreet young
woman regularly looked up at him for his precious approval. He,
in turn, would occasionally give her a stiff little nod. She would
smile blissfully.

Leonard disappeared through that mysterious door and into the
second floor; Wanda began acting as an usherette, guiding the two
guests, in a solemn waltzing step, to the folding chairs whose plain-
ness was disguised by more white bows.

In an effort to preserve the solemnity of this event, it was Wanda's job to separate the sheep from the goats. The sheep were the more formally attired guests; they were ushered to the front. The goats were those inconsiderate people who dressed more informally.

Wanda, who was making quite a name for herself in the celebration business, didn't want the goats to ruin the formal tone of the wedding photos. Of course, Leonard approved.

Leonard's financial analyst and wife, Leonard's accountant and wife, Leonard's computer consultant and wife, Leonard's real estate agent and husband, and finally, Leonard's hairstylist and partner—all formally attired in dark suits or floor-length dresses took up those first rows. They also arrived a few minutes ahead of time. Leonard had trained them well.

Frannie's guests trickled in more casually. Very discreetly but with the severity of the angel of judgment, Wanda ushered them to the back. Once they were deposited there, consigned to the depths, she ignored them as much as possible. Those denizens of the back rows were dressed in the burned-out sixties attire that they usually wore each year to Frannie's August fete. Ralphie, still talking on his cellular phone, walked in with a violet-colored Nehru jacket over patched jeans.

Simon and Jean walked in with furry vests and plastic flowers in their graying hair. Rosemarie came in empty-handed. Wanda had nixed the idea that Rosemarie would cater the event.

Wild mushrooms would certainly not do for this solemn event. In protest, Rosemarie and Theresa wore matching T-shirts, on which were written, "Question Authority!" In fact, all those friends of Frannie who now lived out in the suburbs or in expensive townhouses had dressed with their usual July bash nostalgia. Though those tarnished rebels were dressed for the Revolution, they placidly allowed themselves, under Wanda's authoritative direction, to be ushered to the back chairs. So much for power to the people.

Wanda faced her most difficult decision when Dwayne and Thomas arrived. Thomas was dressed quite formally in a black tuxedo, but Dwayne was dressed in a tie-dyed jeans suite with a lavender scarf around his neck.

Wanda took one look at this couple and made a kind of Sophie's choice. She separated them; Thomas to bask in the honor of those front seats and Dwayne to cast to the outland with the others who she hoped were gnashing their teeth.

Thomas gave Dwayne a silent but rather severe "I told you so nod" and walked with satisfaction toward the front. Dwayne was heard to mutter under his breath. "Where is Rosa Parks when we need her?"

But before that clarion call for justice could instigate some sort of demonstration at the rear, the quiet but tasteful chamber music halted, and the quartette started grinding out strains of some Teutonic march.

This was Wanda's cue to escort Leonard, who appeared now at the front entrance, to the base of the looming grand staircase, which was to be the backdrop for the much awaited ceremony. Once in place, he nodded at Wanda, who returned to her sentinel duty at the door; he then looked up the stairway to receive his bride.

That mysterious now spotlighted door began timidly opening. Finally, that door swung open with impulsive bravado, Frannie flung herself out onto that towering landing. She stood there perched high above the waiting crowd like some rare white bird, her body swathed in yards of white silk; her head veiled with a cloud of lacy mist. For a moment, everyone gasped not so much at her splendor but at the peril she would face descending from those steep stairs all bundled and blinded in white and hobbled with tottering high heels.

The door behind her perfunctorily and unsympathetically closed, cutting off any escape. The quartet stopped. It was clear that Celebrations Inc. had told them to wait for the cue of her first step downward before they could begin the strains of "Here Comes the Bride." That elevated and clouded form tottered and turned around to stare at the closed escape route.

Muffled under all that white, "Oh my" could be heard throughout the hall.

She turned back to face the music and the stairs. The whole veiled form seemed to shudder, then the fingers of her left hand unencumbered by the ponderous bouquet made what looked like desperate snapping motions.

The hall was absolutely silent. That veiled form peered down toward the waiting Leonard. Frozen faced, he raised his left hand slightly and gave a sharp little beckoning gesture.

The form at the top of the stairs lurched and gingerly began its descent—"Here Comes the Bride." Dwayne, who knew that Frannie, didn't even like going down elevators, held his breath, and, for the first time, wondered if getting Frannie together with Leonard was really such a good idea; Frannie kept descending in tiny shaky steps.

At one point, her foot strayed dangerously close to one of the white bouquets in clear glass vases that lined the precipitous edge of the stairway. Her continued unruly descent was threatening to topple that bouquet and send it like a bomb smashing down on the heads on those more formally dressed guests in the front.

Wanda made a quick little hissing sound; Frannie's wayward steps veered back to the center of the stairway. She continued her dangerous journey.

Finally, one step from the bottom, her heel caught on an edge of all that silk, and she tumbled into Leonard's arms. The people in the front rows smiled in polite but evident relief; the people in the back rows cheered.

Ralphie, who had actually put down his cellular phone to pay undivided attention to the hair-raising descent, began whispering into his phone again. "I told her she should have worn her tennis shoes."

Most of all, Leonard was relieved. After all, he had worked so hard to make this event perfect, and it had almost been spoiled.

Very firmly as if nothing had happened, he escorted his bride-to-be to a flower-strewn slightly raised platform, on which a relieved-looking minister waited.

The music had stopped altogether now. As the couple approached the challenge of the dais, Leonard took one step up and whispered to the white form beside him, "Just one more step now." The form gingerly stepped up to the platform. The proceedings began.

Now that the suspense was over, the service droned on with expected questions and expected answers, each guest remembering or wishing or regretting; each waiting for the moment of relief. When the deed was done, the bride revealed, and the kiss placed on her lips, marking the permanence of intent.

The moment came. The bride lifted the veil of mystery, revealing a pale, strained face heightened by makeup. For the briefest of moments, Leonard, who never hesitated except at his mirror in the morning, paused. Perhaps only Wanda who had so carefully and minutely planned this event noticed. Resolutely he kissed the anxious woman newly revealed.

Any misgivings on the part of the married couple were interrupted by the sound of clapping that filled the hall. The music, as if by magic, started up. The people in front began turning to the persons next to them, saying, "What a lovely wedding" or "What a lovely bride!" The people in the back were stunned to see their castanet-clicking queen replaced by a slightly worn-looking fifties bride. At least she didn't break her neck. You know Frannie!

Dwayne snuck up from the back and gave Frannie the second kiss. She seemed stunned under all that white, like someone discovered in a snowstorm. He held her for the slightest moment and felt her body shake.

She glanced at the ring on her hand glimmering in the light of the crystal chandeliers. She returned to the side of her groom, stationing herself there to greet the accountant, financial analyst, real estate agent, computer consultant, hairstylist, and, of course, their respective well-dressed partners.

Wanda was there too, composed and crisply fresh, glowing in the triumph of her celebration. She gave Frannie a sharp little peck on the cheek. Wanda turned to Leonard and for a moment surrendered herself to his grateful and resourceful arms. He reassured her that the hall looked perfect, absolutely perfect. She reassured him that he was more than perfect and then returned to duty, supervising the serving of the little elegant brunch. She had a very busy schedule that day; there was that engagement party out in Minnetonka—such quality people.

While everyone else was becoming bleary with congratulations, the sound of Wanda's hard-edged heels clicked across the ballroom as her hands gave silent but forceful direction to the wait staff. She at

least wore sensible shoes; heels short enough to allow her to maneuver and high enough to give a not unappealing but discreet sway to
those hips of hers that she toned so carefully at the gym. Yes, the
event was perfect even with the complications of the bride.

Frannie's guests, who prided themselves on their informal-
ity, were already charging toward that food-laden table all regaling
themselves with Frannie stories. "Do you remember when…you
know Frannie?"

CHAPTER 11

GENERALLY PEOPLE WANT to forget about a newly married couple as soon as possible. Actually imagining that tuxedoed man and virginal white bride in the messy maneuvers of intercourse can certainly take one aback, but that isn't the primary reason behind that incommunicado period that people call the honeymoon. Rather the purpose of that hazy hidden honeymoon is to discreetly hide those moments when the shiny and almost immortal lovers enter into the gravitational field of ordinary living—grocery shopping, farting, talking too much or not enough, the sound of the beloved eating.

The couple in their archetypal orbit begins to subtly veer toward that anticipated planet of "life as usual." Each astronaut of love belted in separate seats, no longer lovers but crewmembers struggling in tandem to steer that craft into a safe landing. All the while, the atmosphere of reentry rubs against the shield of romantic illusion that had protected them thus far.

Romance begins to burn away until they both plunge into the ocean of ordinary living together, bobbing up and down there waiting for rescue.

Unfortunately, Leonard and Frannie had to wait two months before their prolonged honeymoon in Italy. Leonard was having a difficult time reining in his lawyerly activities; a particularly important case was coming up—one that only Leonard could do.

Still, the two settled into their matrimonial routine in relative privacy. He continued his drive to the top with unabated intensity; he did though curtail his private moments by the mirror.

Frannie, under the directing eye of Leonard, began the task of caring for his house. Her little efforts were perhaps misguided, but indeed, this was part of her charm. If either was disappointed, well, no one else knew it. People tended to keep some distance from the couple's point of impact.

Distance was Leonard's preferred environment anyway, but Frannie wandered around that showcase of a home, wondering why crickets sing so loudly right before the first frost.

Though they were both now living in the same house, the actual meaning of happily ever was, to say the least, miles apart for each other.

Fifteen years ago when his peers were dropping out and protesting in the free-for-all party of the sixties, Leonard was studying hard and planning for his future that certainly didn't include anything about defiance. His life after all was to be devoted to study of law.

While parades of students were taking over the student union, he was studying with an intensity that precluded social contact, not that occasionally he didn't watch those wild-haired hippy girls with longing, the sun in their tresses gleaming as they screamed "Power to the people!" He knew that someday those lotus eaters would realize that he, Leonard Grimbaugh, had the right idea about life. He would show them; he would have it all.

Long before he had actually met Frannie, the new but sharp-eyed junior partner, Thomas, had learned to entertain his otherwise single-minded boss with tales of Dwayne and Frannie hitch-hiking from coast to coast. Thomas was able to combine just the right amount of humor and censure. Though Leonard, of course, was shocked that his business partner was sharing his habitation with someone who must have burned himself out with sex, drugs, and rock and roll; somehow Leonard always wanted to hear more and more of the foolish details.

For Leonard, Frannie had become a dream come true, flashing and smiling and spinning like some lost chance come to life.

On that first afternoon, while he held the tray of hors d'oeuvres, he could imagine himself and Frannie traveling cross-country, hitching rides on Volkswagen vans, sitting around campfires with other witty adventurous free spirits—maybe even, no, that would be too much, ingesting illegal substances. As he watched those long limbs of hers swaying under that absurd skirt, he fell in love.

Unfortunately, Frannie's dreams were steering through rougher waters. She had signed on to a very tight ship indeed.

The house with its myriad precious objects perched precariously on every surface demanded constant care. Very politely, Leonard, the day after the wedding, mentioned that she did not need to bother about most of the house; it was his charge. At first, she sighed with relief; Frannie was far from tidy, and the prospect of having to keep that museum of precious objects clean was daunting. Especially since she had that very morning accidentally knocked over an ever so tiny vase on the bookshelf. She was waiting for the proper moment to tell her spouse.

Though Frannie's now-defunct house had been colorful and quaint, it had also been haphazard. Her flamboyant belongings like broken butterfly wings were pushed untidily into boxes. She wondered if she would ever see them again let alone need them; she had Leonard and a new life now.

Yes, she did need to tell Leonard about that little vase yet. She waited until the evening after she cooked her famous tuna casserole a la Frannie. She just knew how much he liked it. She opened up the conversation. "How wonderful to spend absolutely every evening with you, my dear."

Leonard looked over his glasses at her very benignly.

"My Leonard, you certainly seem to take care of things so well, but I need to do something while I live here. Perhaps the bathroom? Oh, by the way, when I picked out a copy of *Pride and Prejudice* from your bookshelf this morning, I accidentally knocked over a tiny, little vase." She smiled with an innocent pout of an apology.

He continued to look over his glasses, benevolence draining from his face. He shook his head as if perhaps he had misunderstood her.

There was a gap of silence.

Finally, Frannie said, "I love the way you take care of things. Everything is so lovely, really. It was only that little old vase tucked away in the corner of the shelf."

As the information sunk in about the unexpected change in the fortunes of his house, for an instant, his eyes shot open in either rage or terror. Then with remarkable determination, his eyelids squeezed together to a slit, and his face froze to contain the explosion inside.

Face masked, he began speaking with a stiff formality. "Frannie…" There was a long pause. "Do you mean the small blue vase on the second shelf…the Tiffany vase?"

She looked up at Leonard with as much innocence as she could still muster. Then she tilted her head down. "Little clumsy old me."

"It's one of a kind, Frannie. That little old vase is one of a kind." As he said *one*, his eyes flared wildly. Something bitter spilled out.

Frannie stopped batting her eyes. All coyness drained from her face, and her pale features began turning red. "Oh dear, I'm so sorry, Leonard. I really am. I guess sometimes I just don't notice things."

He was back in control again. His burning eyes were embedded in the mask of his frozen face. "Yes, I had planned to talk with you about that. Things *are* important, Frannie. You certainly should be old enough to understand that."

The words clipped out of his tight lips like the sound of keys punched on a computer.

He turned away from her.

"I really am sorry, Leonard, really." Her head dropped to shield herself. Then she looked up at him, trying to plead for mercy.

She succeeded in getting his attention. He turned his bitter eyes to her. "Yesterday," he said the word with emphasis like he was pleading a case for the prosecution, "when I put the dishes away that you washed after supper, I found debris on some of the items, little remnants of food, around the rim of the saucepan, on the underside of a fork, and even on my silver platter." With each item that he mentioned, his voice struck a deeper chord of reproach. Then he paused, his point proven.

This conversation was not turning out the way she planned. There was no final exasperated but good-natured "you know, Frannie" ending. She looked away in confusion.

This evasion only steeled Leonard's purpose. "Do you hear me, Frannie? We cannot live with that kind of carelessness."

How strange to be cornered with no escape. How very strange. Though her head remained down, something surprising and unusual seemed to be churning in her body, finally coiling its way up her spine. Whatever was happening reached her neck; her head shot up. "Why do you fill your house with all those knickknacks anyway?"

For a second, his face went limp with shock. The enemy had broken through his barricade and was living in his home. His face twisted in terror for a moment. Determined person that he was, he prepared for the intruder. Words clipped out of his tight lips as fast as machine gun bullets. "Knickknacks? So that's what you think about my house and me? That was a one of a kind Tiffany vase. Look around yourself, Frannie. Look around real well. This is not the kind of trash that you are used to. This is the real thing. Now you insult me after I took you in. Is this the kind of behavior that I can expect of you?" He stared at her.

There she was, left with the unaccustomed mess of her anger. Her body heated with embarrassment. How could she have lost her temper? How could she have allowed herself to say something nasty? She peeked up out of her embarrassment up at his blistering outrage. She noticed how his hands were twitching, scratching, almost clawing at his legs. Why, all weren't lost; he was simply afraid.

She, Frannie Fortunato, would be the person to comfort him. "Oh, I didn't mean that, Leonard. Your things are so beautiful. I just love them. It's just once in a while…once in a while, there are just so many of them…I just get afraid sometimes that I'll break them."

"What do you mean, Frannie, *so many of them*? There you go again, Frannie, always trying to blame me. And then you yell at me." The mask of his face loosened slightly into a pout.

She heard the change in his voice, not exactly softness but at least something not completely impermeable. She looked up; she just knew that he was really just crying out for help.

Now this was a role with which she was more comfortable. That anger of hers was just a little mistake. "Oh, my dear, I didn't mean that there were too many. Why I admire your taste? Everyone does. I'm just not used to your home yet. Your things are lovely, and you take such good care of them. I am so lucky to be able to live here." She almost meant it.

He saw the weakness in his foe. "How can I ever believe you again, Frannie, or trust you when you attack me like this? You hurt me, Frannie. You really did." That face of his continued to melt into a pout.

For a moment, that funny thing started to happen at the base of her spine again. For the slightest moment, she wanted to scream at him, but then she noticed how a little tremor seemed to be shaking his body. Why, that big strong man needed her sympathy, her kindness, and most of all her care. He was her Leonard after all. She stilled anything uncomfortable coming up from inside her and began speaking with an overwhelmingly sympathetic tone, "Oh, my dear, dear Leonard." Then she touched his face.

He gave off a little whimper. "You yelled at me, Frannie, you really did."

She had found a way out. "I'm sorry, Leonard. I didn't mean to raise my voice. I don't know what got into me. I suppose all these changes have been hard on me."

His face tightened a little. "Are you saying that I haven't tried hard enough?"

"Oh no, Leonard, I know you're trying so hard, and this must be so difficult for you." The word *you* trailed off with heartfelt, sympathetic abandon.

He made a little sniffling sound. "I've tried to make you feel comfortable here. I think of you all the time. I'm always trying to make you happy."

She loved that wounded pleading look on men's face. Why, everything was going to be all right after all.

She fingered her ring, feeling the smoothness and warmth of the gold and then the sharp facets of that glittering stone. He was her boy now. "I know how hard you're trying, Lenny. Sometimes I don't think." She touched him on the back of his neck and rubbed away the last of his fierceness.

"I'm so afraid of losing you, Frannie."

"I know."

They moved toward the mammal warmth that each other offered: to safety in a world that seemed so dangerous. Yes, everything was better now.

* * *

In the dark of that night when she lay in those sheets that always seemed clean, she felt his hands gently, gratefully touch those embarrassingly small breasts of hers—such devotion. Her husband worshipped at the altar of herself, now sucking her nipples with absolute reverence. But all the time, she felt the wild power of his body pressing into her as if at any moment he could be unleashed and thrust into her with cruel abandon.

His lips were on hers now. His moist fleshy tongue, with a life of its own, was thrusting, exploring the mystery that any opening afforded him. For a mount she could barely breathe, her mouth plugged and the full weight of his body pushing ever harder. Just as he thrust his thick cock between her legs and into herself, she noticed that the smell of his breath was sour. Then her body started responding almost on its own to the force of being needed. She heard herself silently whisper, "Don't be a baby, Frannie. Everything is all right."

His voice, choked with passion, said, "What did you say, Frannie?"

"Oh, just that everything is all right."

He gasped and pushed harder into her. "All right, all right, *all right*."

She felt his cock throb and then empty into her. She caressed his back with careful, artful hands.

CHAPTER 12

ON THOSE MID-SEPTEMBER afternoons with Leonard away at work, before she started planning some kind of supper, she would sit in a tiny room that she called her own. It's true that the stiff Victorian sofa and the large ornate bookcase loaded with precious artifacts were Leonard's, but still, there was room on the narrow space of the floor for a few piles of the extravagant flimsy remnants of her former life. In fact, on those afternoons when the sun still had warmth, which blew through the window screen, she would sit on the floor, barricaded from Leonard's world by the remains of her past.

The geography of her former chaos had shrunken dramatically. What yesterday had filled a whole house, spilling over in its abundance to the Veterans Home and onto her amused friends, had now been constrained to this tiny room, one thin wall away from Leonard's study. True, he was gone during the day, but it did seem after that little misunderstanding of theirs, and it really was just a misunderstanding that he was spending shorter days at the office and more time at home.

He had such acute hearing. Three rooms away, he could hear a disappointed sigh. As for phone calls, he might as well be on the phone with her. Last time she talked to Dodo, he even asked her why she was whispering.

You'd think hearing as much as Leonard did, he would develop some sort of sense of humor, but alas, his resourcefulness was always at a fever pitch.

True, occasionally, he would release a ratchety, high-pitched squeal when no one else was around, and he was particularly pleased with Frannie's charm. But there was no sense of flippant irony, no appreciation of exaggeration, as if everything said was a statement to be meticulously cross-examined.

And Frannie was the mistress of exaggeration, turning the most casual encounter into a brush with death. And death was to be met with dancing.

Several evenings later would Leonard was busily typing at his computer, Frannie called Dodo. She got all the mileage she could out of the description of her latest culinary fiasco. Dodo, as usual, said that Thomas didn't listen to him anymore. Then there was nothing for them to say to each other.

That Thursday, they had even missed their afternoon at the Cracked Cup. They just didn't seem to have that much to talk about anymore. They both sat in their respective homes, holding the dull dead phone with nothing to say but afraid to hang up. There was something so final about hanging up.

Frannie ended that silence. "You know, men, Dodo, can't live with them, and you can't live without them."

"Yeah, DeeDee. Thank god we're the fairer sex."

"Well, at least one of us is."

"Since when have you become such a stickler for details? Besides, my feet are smaller."

"My breasts are bigger."

"Just barely."

"Don't rub it in."

"Well, DeeDee, back to the men in our lives!"

"By Dodo."

She put the phone down and walked to the next room just to see if Leonard was all right. She had a habit now of checking on him, especially after she had talked with one of her friends. This time, when she entered Leonard's study, he had already stopped typing.

"Hi, honey, I just talked with Do—I mean—Dwayne. We have our little chats, you know."

Leonard was as silent as a stone.

"You know how it is."

Leonard obviously didn't.

"Are you all right, my dear? How about a cup of tea?"

Silence again. Suddenly, his eyes flashed out of that mask of his, and his lips began moving with precision. "Frannie, how could you do that?"

Her body did a quick little defensive jerk. "Is something wrong?" She began rubbing her ring. "Isn't the bathroom clean enough?"

"How could you talk to my business associate's partner like that? Violating my privacy by insinuating something was wrong between us."

"Wrong?"

"You know what I mean, Frannie. I'll quote, 'You know, men can't live with them, can't live without them.' Who else would you be talking about...but me?"

"Oh, Leonard, that's a joke. Everybody says that."

"Everybody?"

"I don't know...I suppose not everybody...but it's just one of those things that you kind of say when you don't have any more to say."

"So, Frannie, it's one of the things you say about me."

"Oh, I'm sorry, I mean, I didn't mean it that way. I didn't mean to hurt you."

"If you say that in the house when I'm here, what do you say when I'm away? This is where I live. Did you think about what it's like for me to know that you are saying critical insulting things under my very own roof? Think of me for once, Frannie."

Her chest was heaving up and down; her body seemed to be doing that funny twisting from the spine again. With some new source of determination, she seemed to steel herself against whatever was happening on the inside. For a moment, a funny blank expression passed over her face that almost mirrored his.

He watched her and seemed troubled. "I love you, Frannie. How dare you go away like this!"

Her blank expression faded, and whatever had been pulsing inside was stilled. She looked charming and sympathetic again. "I'm sorry for hurting you." She was now sidling up to him, rubbing his neck. "Oh, Lenny, you're my man, my big strong man. What would I do without you?"

Her touch seemed to soften something inside him.

Then he stiffened again. "I want you to promise me, Frannie, that you won't talk about our relationship on the phone anymore. All right?"

She was busy calming him now, rubbing his shoulders. "How could I refuse you anything, my darling? I really wasn't trying to hurt you, but I'll be more careful."

"Frannie." Even though his voice was severe, his body was relaxing and perhaps just beginning to respond to the pleasure of safety.

She could feel him and how she moved him. His breathing was no longer tight and rapid but was beginning to heave through his whole body.

"Everything is going to be just fine, Leonard. How could I not love you, my dear man?"

Words weren't necessary any longer. His arousal was in charge.

For a few moments, she could forget everything. She knew she pleased him. It was all so simple now. Just the feeling safe, the feeling of being held on to, all the while holding out. Though his arms circled her, she was shrinking into a spooky fluttering place inside herself that he could never enter, let alone contain, the place for which she did not have words. How crucial that fluttery place, now that her other escapes were gone. He led her to the bedroom.

His stubbly cheeks pressed against her; his tongue once again found its way into her mouth, and then he said, "You're wonderful, Frannie," and began throwing off his clothes like some excited boy. She took off her clothes more carefully. He was already in bed, watching her by the time she was down to her panties and bra. His large penis stood erect with an occasional little quiver.

He loved to watch her. She undid her bra and ever so slowly lowered her panties, unsure if she was drawing out his pleasure or simply buying time. Then she lowered herself into his arms and, for a moment, was absolutely still. He placed his hands on her buttocks and rolled over on top of her. She smiled charmingly at him. He pressed against her and then thrust into her body, intent as a Boy Scout. She was somewhere else.

That spooky place with no name inside her self-offered much more latitude than the breadth of Leonard's insistent arms. This evening, she found herself remembering the first time she had gone to a circus.

She was there with her friend Betty Sue. She and Betty Sue used to spend whole summers blowing bubbles in their secret place made from a blanket thrown over the picnic table.

At the end of one of those summers, her father brought them to a real circus. She loved the clowns and the tigers and the beautiful women riding, standing up on horses, but mostly she loved the way there were three separate rings to watch.

When it got too scary watching the men flying on the trapeze, suddenly, clowns and dogs would be doing funny tricks in the next ring. Even the scariest moment didn't seem too scary because soon something altogether different would be happening somewhere else. Sometimes and Frannie liked this the best, all three rings would be going on at the same time. She could look from one ring to the other and then to the other. She was never scared that way.

For a moment, she returned to Leonard. In the ring of his arms, he was thrusting deeper and deeper into her with that determined cock of his. His tongue was pushing into the ring of her mouth. Ah, but the third ring was safe.

In that third ring, somewhere in the vicinity of her heart, there was spooky darkness—such a good place to hide. What a clever girl she was. She gasped an "Oh my!"

Leonard, who presumed that she was being transported to new heights of pleasure by his lovemaking, said, "It's all right, Frannie. Don't hold back. Just relax and go there."

She did. Though her body throbbed under his attention, she was in a different place, watching the shadows move in the third ring.

The next morning, the alarm went off; Leonard's body in repose startled with a jerk.

The battle of his life was resuming. Then he heard her soft breath rising and falling next to him, whispering like soft seas of comfort. For an instant, the vigilance of his body melted into the sound of her breath. He felt the warmth of her contained under the covers, the warmth of her dreams, those mysterious dreams. And she was his to care for and protect and most certainly enjoy.

He breathed in the pleasure of that last night like some adventurous boy exploring a new land that opened and emptied out just for him, like a treasure...Frannie.

In the light of morning, her face was slack, and the skin on her neck seemed dry like parchment; but still, she was his treasure, his reason to keep pushing ahead. How he loved those moments in the morning when she lay next to him.

He pushed up on his elbow and hovered above her, drank in her breathing presence before placing a soft kiss on that morning cheek of hers.

With her eyes closed, she made a kind of humming sound, and the corners of her lips turned up in a smile. Her eyes cracked open slightly and then opened wide with a little fluttering tremor. She flashed a groggy smile at him. "Why don't I get up and make you breakfast and see you off, my darling?"

He still hung above her, watching the play of her face. "Oh, honey, you stay in bed now. I love to see you look so content. It's better than a cup of coffee. I'll remember you like this all day." He rested his hand on her cheek. "You will watch that phone business, won't you, Frannie?"

For a moment, her face tensed into that charming, dissembling look that he had grown to dislike so much. She sensed his displeasure and smoothed it over into apologetic submission. "How could I refuse you anything, my dear?"

CHAPTER 13

LEONARD HAD SO much to do.

As he showered, he pictured the list of all the things he needed to perfectly accomplish that day. He loved lists. How could anything be more beautiful than those numbered words all carefully written down in order of precedence simply waiting to direct him? Once a task was written, he performed it with exemplary skill and to perfection.

He was soaping the not-so-exemplary folds of his body, brushing over the coarse hair of his chest. He felt a moment of incongruent repugnance. His soapy hand pushed at his hairy stomach, beginning to pouch out and obscure his maleness. And his maleness seemed so diminished this morning barely peeking out from the fold at the bottom of his stomach.

He took the soap and rubbed earnestly on his expanding belly and diminishing penis, and then he slightly lifted one leg and rubbed the soap down and under, around to his anus. He looked up furtively. Then the warmth of the water, the silkiness of the soap, and the roughness of his hand created unexpected friction on that hanging flaccid cock of his. His hand began clutching and kneading that flesh dangling out of his hairy crotch. His face lost that frightened intensity and softened into a deeper almost luxurious breathing. He thought of Frannie sleeping in the next room. His cock and his whole lower body came to unexpected life, and for a moment, he was young—young as he had never been.

Fears and resourceful lists paled, leaving his mind and his whole body open pleasure. *Oh*, how he loved her, his treasure beyond all worth.

As he rapidly toweled himself off, his list of duties again materialized. Normally his showers were brisk urgent affairs—the first thing on his list.

This morning, he was in the shower long enough to mist over the bathroom mirror. There in the mirror, instead of the vaguely haunted figure he was used to seeing, he saw a large powerful male shape, details misted over, romanticized. It took him a moment to recognize himself.

He smiled at the hazy image. He glanced suspiciously from side to side.

Once again, his face hardened, and he set off to confront the world. He rushed back into his bedroom to throw on his clothes hardly noticing the still form on the bed. Feet were thrust into his shoes; laces were tied in quick precise motions. Done. His heels clicked into the bathroom. He combed that thinning hair of his in the clearing mirror and then rushed down the stairs.

Yes, he would listen to the Italian language tapes on the way to work, give his receptionist the flight numbers and dates of his trip, fax the hotel in Rome, review the Frasier case with Thomas, get one last haircut, meet Wanda at Damico's—that was the least he could do since she volunteered to bring them to the airport. How thoughtful and organized she was: meet with the entire office staff to check that they were all prepared for his departure and call the house sitter to make sure that he didn't have any last-minute questions.

He wondered with a hint of irritation if Frannie was still in bed. When they got back from Italy, he would need to see that she found something to do with her time. Not that he minded that she didn't plan for things, but for her sake, she would need to have something to do. Yes, he'd talk with Wanda about it. She had such good ideas. If only Frannie would think a little more.

Two hours later, Frannie was preparing for a trip too. She was sitting in that little room of hers, wondering just what clothes she could bring, certainly plenty of long skirts. She could almost see herself dancing under the romantic Italian moon, Signora Frannie. Though she couldn't speak a word of Italian, she just knew she would be among kindred spirits. After all, wasn't Italy the home of castanets and flamingo dancing, or was that Spain? Oh my!

Outside the closed window, the rain-soaked tree bark had turned black, and the leaves on the ground that had been fragrant and gold yesterday were transformed into messy slime. Thank god the heat was on, although Leonard kept it much, much too low.

She was sitting in that house, fingers feeling just a nip of chill, beginning to wonder what she actually would do in Italy for three whole months.

At least she would escape the cold dark winter; after all, they would be on the sunny Mediterranean…yes, in some sunbaked village that smelled of garlic and basil.

People would be living at a pace she understood. Every morning, she would wake to the warmth and promise of that Italian sun. Leonard would be there beside her, very relaxed; that strange frozen look of his melted away by the carefree warmth. They would have coffee sitting on a veranda overlooking the quiet turquoise sea.

As bells rang in the limpid valley below, donkeys would be making their way into town loaded down with produce for the extravagant supper that she would make that evening. She would expand her cooking repertoire. Leonard would be amazed and proud of her.

Perhaps it was the thought of cooking, but her reverie was interrupted by that nagging question again: "Frannie, what would you actually do for all those months?"

Too much time was a bit of a problem now, although she would never admit that to Leonard. No casual phone calls in Italy. Suddenly, she remembered that little phone problem last night. She *would* have to be more careful at least a little.

In Italy, she wouldn't have this little room that in the last two months had become chaotic enough to make her feel a little more comfortable. Even though she was sure that she would be surrounded by kindred spirits in Italy, still, she couldn't talk to anybody.

She had attempted to listen to some Italian lessons on tape but kept falling asleep. She wouldn't be able to have her friends over, although this too had become difficult lately. How Leonard positively hated to have her friends drop by.

If he knew ahead of time, he would rush around frantically polishing tables and dusting his bric-a-brac. When her friends came to the door, he would greet them with an icy little smile, very formally pronouncing every syllable of every word just a little too clearly.

There was no hanging around with Leonard. Under his critical eye, her guests tended to talk about the weather or perhaps the state of the economy and then leave quickly.

There was always something that they just remembered that they had to do. When they left, Leonard would start asking his questions, not to get more information but in a strange disapproving complaint.

If her friends came by unbidden, oh, how she used to love surprises. Well, then she really had something to face. On the guest's unexpectedly speedy departure, Leonard would start cross-examining her with unrelenting reproach: "Did you notice the way that your friends only talked to you and totally, totally ignored me?"

"Ignored you? No, I really didn't notice. I did notice that they were quieter than usual."

"Did you see the way Jean contemptuously brushed away the bowl of peanuts that I offered her as if it wasn't good enough for her?"

"Oh, Leonard, she had just eaten a little earlier. If it was chocolate, she would have devoured all of it including the bowl and your fingers. Jean loves chocolate so."

"There you are defending them again. How could you let them treat me that way?"

She found herself backing away, her whole body beginning to coil. "Oh, *Leonard,* they were trying to be friendly, but you wouldn't talk to them."

"Don't raise your voice to me, Frannie. Here I am simply asking questions, and you start screaming at me. I work hard all day, and when I come home, I have to put up with abuse. I saw the way you all looked at me."

Frannie could feel the pressure building inside him; she tried to switch gears. "Oh, my dear, I'm sorry it was so hard for you. Everything is going to be all right, I promise. My friends don't dislike you."

"'Don't dislike me.' I know what that means. You like them more than you like me, and they just put up with me."

Now she could hear her heart pounding. "Leonard, I love you, you're my husband. Don't do this to me please."

"Frannie, you're the one whose doing something, bringing in people who insult me."

Her eyes began smoldering. "They were not insulting you."

His face became absolutely rigid except for the crack that had been his mouth. "Is this the kind of behavior I have to expect from your guests? Is this the kind of behavior I have to expect from you? This is betrayal, Frannie."

Frannie found herself squirming again and none too charmingly. "*My* guest! At least I have friends. You think friendship is having your accountant and consultants and your real estate agent over for stupid cocktails once a year while you fuss over them. I didn't even mention that jerky little Wanda. She probably starches her tampons!"

He looked at her, eyes burning, staring her down in bitter silence.

For a moment, she stood him off with her own fierceness, and then something inside, some sort of resolve started eroding; and once again, she slipped into apology. "Oh, Leonard, I shouldn't have said that about your friends even Wanda. I'm sorry. I'm getting carried away. I'm sure you know a lot about friendship."

Leonard, from years of practice, could see that the witness was crumbling. He moved in for the kill. "The truth finally comes out. You stand in my house and tell *me* how I should live my life. You insult me in *my* house. Frannie, you're a judgmental, violent person. Don't you see how terribly you are treating me after all I've done for you?"

Frannie's face prickled with hot shame. All her old strategies seemed so useless. Her resolve was slipping. Perhaps she was doing something terribly wrong; perhaps she really was a violent person. Didn't all his friends say that Leonard was always right? He was so smart and so good to her. Her head dropped down in doubtful silence.

Leonard knew that he had won; he always won. Now finally was the time for mercy. "Oh, Frannie, can't you see that I love you even with all your faults?" He paused for a moment. She was crying. Something in him softened. How he loved to take care of her when she cried.

"I know you do, Leonard. I just get so confused sometimes."

"That's why I'm here, my love."

She moved over to him and touched his hand. She lifted it up to her lips and kissed it silently. "You're so good to me, Leonard."

"Now, Frannie," he stopped his slide into eroticism for a moment, "I want you to promise me to try harder with your friends. I know that they are important to you, but after all, I am your husband. Now you can still have your friends over…sometimes, but you have to make sure that they treat me politely."

She was in the second ring of her own private circus now; she was fervently even a little desperately caressing his wrist and arm. "Oh, my dear Leonard." She could hear his breathing slow.

While Leonard was making love to her that night, out of the blue, she began thinking about her friend Mona. Mona.

Blue. It was a blue warm day on the Pacific coast. Dodo and DeeDee were sitting on their backpacks by the side of the coastal road below San Francisco on the road through the Big Sur.

It was late morning, and they were eating two of the last three peanut butter trail cookies. A car stopped near them and very unceremoniously deposited a rather short dark-haired woman dressed in a plaid shirt and jeans so worn that they were stretched out of shape. She had the look of someone who had been one the road for a considerable time.

She walked over the two. "That prick wouldn't leave me alone. How many times do I have to tell a guy I don't want to fuck him? My name's Mona."

Frannie was so impressed with the stranger that she offered her the very last cookie.

The three sat there, eating to the sound of seagulls. Then they wiped their hands as thoroughly as they could on their pants, and in a casual newfound togetherness stuck out their thumbs.

After twenty minutes, the three decided to postpone geographic travel and start out on a different kind of journey; they walked down to the misty ocean and dropped acid. Soon they were completely engrossed in the bizarre world contained in the little plot of sand, on which they were sitting.

Waves crawled up the beach like playful kittens—all blue and white and gold and fuchsia.

The three eventually found themselves naked and kissing each other as they crawled to join the kittens. Then in a psychedelic transformation, they suddenly became one large luxurious kitten licking itself.

Frannie felt Leonard's body make one last desperate thrust into her. As his body began quivering, she held him reassuringly. Yes, she must call Mona tomorrow.

The next afternoon, while Frannie was sure that Leonard was particularly preoccupied at the office, she made her call. "Hey, Mona, hi."

"Hey, De, I was just thinking about you. How's matrimonial bliss?"

"Oh, it's all right…just fine, it really is."

"Trouble in paradise?"

"How are you? What makes you say that?"

"My plant business is slow, Kathy is away, and I'm premenstrual. Other than that, fairly well. Whenever you sound like you're trying to convince me of something, I know there's trouble."

"Trouble…you think so?"

"Frannie, it's your life, not mine. How are you?"

"So business is pretty slow."

"Can you believe it, it's Berkeley, and people aren't interested in buying house plants?"

"Maybe they're not smoking enough marijuana. Oops, I shouldn't have said that. You being in a twelve-step program and all."

"I still have a sense of humor, Frannie, just not a habit anymore."

"How are you doing with Kathy?"

"You know, women, can't live with them, and can't live without them."

"Sounds familiar."

"We had this big fight before she left to visit her mother in Pasadena. She just assumed that I'd love to feed her cats, dogs, parakeets, and fish while she was away. I was planning to go to a soul retrieval workshop in Santa Barbara."

"I didn't know you lost it."

"I didn't. I'm learning a new skill. Do you think people are actually smoking less?"

"I don't know. I still want to find out what soul retrieval is."

"I'm planning to supplement my income by doing body work. Soul retrieval is a way to help a person find parts of herself that she abandoned in childhood."

"Do you think it works?"

"Beats me. I guess that's why I decided to let Therese go, and I'm left with the menagerie. I suppose I should really go to a codependency workshop."

"My, there seems to be a group for everything."

"I'm tired of talking about my shit. Let's cut to the chase. What's wrong, Frannie?"

"You know me. Things are all right…any earthquakes recently?"

"Cut the shit. What's up?"

"Oh, I always get by. You know that. Do you remember when we hitchhiked? There was always that moment when you wonder if you'll ever get another ride?"

"So you're having a hard time."

"Oh, I suppose so."

"Speak to me."

"Well, you asked for it. You know how so many women would jump at the chance to have someone so resourceful taking care of them?"

"I suppose some women want that. Seems pretty weird to me, although I'm not into penises. I always did wonder why you were looking for some guy to take care of you. There you were bright and

creative, leading Dodo, boy wonder, around the country, still wanting to be sleeping beauty or something."

"It's not that bad, is it?"

"It's not bad, Frannie. I just could never figure out why you
were doing it."

"You make me feel like an idiot or something."

"It's not that at all. I just wondered why you always seemed to
be waiting around for something to happen, like you never could
actually finish anything because you were waiting for whatever you
hoped would happen to happen."

"There you go again. Just because I wouldn't move in with you
and live in Berkeley—"

"Eat shit!"

There was a pause on Frannie's end of the line. "Well, I was just
sitting here and thought I'd give you a call. I'll be leaving for Italy
next week for three months."

"I always get dizzy when we talk on the phone. Let me sit down
here."

"Feel free."

"Sure, I had a crush on you back then, but that ended a long
time ago. Besides, we would have driven each other nuts if we
lived together."

"Yeah?"

"So you're leaving for Italy soon."

"Well, you see, Mona, things are a little testy here. I really am
lucky that Leonard loves me, but sometimes, well, he's so busy prov-
ing the point that I feel like he just doesn't listen to me. Sometimes I
feel I'm kind of stuck here, maybe for good. He really is good to me,
but he seems angry with me a lot."

"Angry a lot?"

"Well, at first, it was kind of endearing the way he always
wanted my attention. He really doesn't want other people around me
too much. I felt like I could fly into his arms. I even gave up my job.
I would have had to anyway because we're going on this long trip.
But sometimes I feel like something really is closing in on me, and
there's no way out."

"Oh, De, I'm sorry. I always thought of you as this multicol-ored butterfly landing on flowers for just a few seconds and then flying off, not superficial exactly, but it's just part of your nature to fly off quickly."

"Am I really like that? Flitting around all the time? Is that really how I seem to you?"

"Is this a game of truth or dare? Let's put it this way. You're my dear friend, but when the going gets rough, you get going."

"So you want to change me too? I should become some sort of a marine."

"Okay, okay, hold your horses. I haven't stayed friends with you all these years, hoping to change you into another person. Frannie Fortunato is just fine by me. I think what I really meant was that you seem like you have this incredible knack for getting out of tight spots. Sometimes I wonder what would happen if you couldn't get away so easily."

"So this is your fault."

"Maybe finally getting caught by a situation is one of the joys of middle age."

"That sounds ominous. Can't I just pretend I'm twenty?"

"Pretending only goes so far."

"Now you tell me. Maybe you've lost your sense of humor? You sound suspiciously like the new and improved Dwayne the therapist."

Silence on the other end of the phone.

"Okay so I feel like this stupid middle-aged butterfly in a net."

"Sorry about that."

"Really? Or are you just saying that to prove you're right about me?"

"Bitch."

"I love it when you talk dirty to me."

"There's 900 numbers for that."

"Okay, okay. I guess I called you because I'm feeling in a sort of mess. It's not that I'm exactly sure I want to get out, but I'm also not exactly sure I could if I wanted to."

"Makes sense to me."

"It does?"

"Sure."

"Well, Mona, you see it's something like this. Leonard and I are going to Italy, and there won't be anyone else around. Of course, Leonard has all kinds of lists of things to do. I don't know what I'll do. I can't even speak Italian."

"Why don't you take up knitting or something? Besides, from what I hear of winter in Italy, you'll need all the sweaters you can get."

"Isn't it supposed to be sunny and warm in Italy?"

"Not in winter, sorry to give you the bad news. Grimbaugh sounds like a real treat."

"Oh, I don't know, I suppose it'll be all right. He really is kind to me."

"So knitting doesn't sound like it'll work. Hmm, Kathy is forever journaling. Whenever we get caught in one of our fights that don't go anywhere, she goes to her room and writes. Hey, why don't you try it, even though I'm still pissed at her for leaving me with all these fucking animals? Might help you when you're feeling caught, you know, you wouldn't slam your wings to shreds as much."

"Oh yeah? You know how I hate to write. I sound like a boring idiot. I can just imagine it now. 'This morning, I saw the picturesque coliseum. What a magnificent sight! I had a pizza today.'"

"Sounds like one of your postcards."

"People aren't supposed to read postcards. Just look at the picture on the other side."

"Now you tell me."

"My postcards really sound like that? I always thought they were kind of witty."

"Why don't you write postcards to yourself, except there won't be any pictures on the other side?"

"What's the point if there are no pictures?"

"Okay, okay, I won't press the point. It's just an option."

"Okay, I'll think about it. No promises."

"No promises."

"Well, I better get to the store. I've got this recipe book called *The Instant Gourmet*. I'm making beef stroganoff for Leonard tonight, except I use cream of mushroom soup instead of all that complicated other stuff."

"I know how you like cream of mushroom soup."

"Well, thanks anyway, Mona."

"Write me when you get an address."

"Sure."

"The force be with you."

"Swell."

That afternoon, Frannie escaped from Leonard's house, flitting from store to store on Grand Avenue. Besides picking up cream of mushroom soup for stroganoff a la Frannie, she stopped at a card store to pick up postcards.

She loved to send cards. She could get someone's attention without having to organize her thoughts.

There by the checkout counter was a rack of writing notebooks each with a different picture on the cover—a lady slipper and football players and cartoon characters and even one with a picture of the world seen from outer space.

She simply couldn't resist the incongruity of that selection. She bought four of them—one of each picture. She even picked out a pink pen.

CHAPTER 14

THAT NIGHT AFTER the beef stroganoff a la Frannie, which Leonard seemed to deeply appreciate, although he did mention that Wanda was taking a course in gourmet cooking, the couple exercised their prerogatives in bed: Leonard taking charge and Frannie being taken charge, after which Leonard quickly fell asleep.

Unfortunately, Frannie couldn't find that comfortable position that would allow her the satisfaction of relaxing into sleep. She carefully turned from side to side, afraid to wake her sleeping spouse; he worked so hard after all.

When she did find a position where her nose didn't itch or her right hip didn't ache, her mind was bombarded with vivid snapshots that moved through her brain so quickly that she couldn't focus. It felt like falling.

She separated from those flashing pictures long enough to know that she was uncomfortable… my, she certainly was. She opened her eyes to the shadowed darkness—yes, that wasn't so bad—and listened for a moment to the regular whispers and snufflings of Leonard's breath.

Then and there she discovered quite easily and perhaps even brilliantly that she didn't have to stay in bed.

Moving ever so slowly, so as not to disturb the regularity of his sleep, she turned to face the outside edge of the bed. First, she cautiously slid toward that escape route. Then she began pushing her legs forward until her toes began to peak out from underneath the covers. Her upper torso, almost on its own, began slowly tilting upward. She carefully shifted the covers so that the warmth and security of Leonard's dreams would not be lost into the chilly night. She was sitting up now. The chilly floor nipped her toes, and the air seemed brisk like morning. She felt downright mischievous, like when she and Dodo would start out on a hitchhiking trip with miles of adventure ahead. How amazed she always was to realize that she could travel all the way across country simply standing by the road and sticking out her thumb.

Slowly she shifted her weight from her buttocks to her feet to the chilly floor. Leonard snorted a little, and the rhythm of his breath was interrupted. She froze in position. His breaths fell back into their steadier pace. She stood up naked as the moment of her birth, hardly disturbing that conjugal bed, and delicately stepped out of that confinement and into adventure. She moved as softly as a secret.

The night murmured to Frannie, a car drove by outside, one of the stairs creaked out a complaint, the furnace fan hummed, and of course, her breath whispered exciting secrets—this was an adventure.

She was moving around in the dark now—a dark that no longer was just an empty place but promised surprises. Odd how she felt comfortable as if, well, as if she was no longer in Leonard's house.

Her mind wasn't just slipping away into a memory, but this seemed a real geographic place somehow transformed by the magic of night.

Her feet seemed to direct her on with an easy determination. Yes, they knew where she wanted to be. She slipped into that tiny room that was hers and closed the door ever so quietly. Let there be light!

Suddenly, the chaotic variety that had been her life burst into view. She was standing in its midst now. Opening a dresser drawer, she pulled out warm socks from the tumble of clothes there. Then she walked to her closet and slipped on the very same purple dress, in which she had met Leonard. Her hand brushed against a shawl with elephants, and stars stamped on it. She threw it around her shoulders and for a moment quietly snapped her castanets.

Now she was ready, but ready for what? She stood quietly for a whole minute.

A few months ago, she would have made a long-distance call to Mona or turned on music downstairs and danced or picked dry leaves off her hanging Swedish ivy; instead her options were severely limited—limited to this room in which she must remain very quiet.

She listened for the sound of Leonard's breathing two rooms away. Yes, he was still asleep. He would worry if he woke without her presence next to him.

She sat down on that Victorian sofa in the cool of night to ponder. Now pondering was something that Frannie seldom did; she seldom, at least in her former life, had the spare time.

The chaos that had been her home did not really signify messiness; rather it was an indication of the absolute flurry in which she lived the kind of flurry where things seemed to spin around on their own.

On that softly whispering night with Leonard sleeping and the whirl of her activities strangely still, on this deep silent night, she waited in this room that wasn't even her own, waited not tensely, but rather like a child in front of some deep shadowed pool, a curious child.

There sitting next to her, humming as softly as the furnace, sat those four notebooks. Now normally Frannie had the habit of buying things, bright things which she might fancy but surely never use. By the time she would have carried home whatever doodads that had intrigued her, her life would have already taken several turns away from what had first intrigued her. She would drop those fascinations into the picturesque maelstrom of her house.

She didn't have that geographic luxury now. Those bright tablets that she had deposited in the room just sat there on the sofa, refusing to budge, as if she actually was supposed to do something with them. She stared at Mickey Mouse, a lady slipper, a charging football player, and the round blue earth—they seemed to beckon her, almost nagged at her.

In that tiny room, in the solitude of night, she faced an unusual dilemma; some immediate action, which she had not cajoled from the future, seemed needed. She sat there with the silent urgency of a flower bud, something secret happening, creeping up from the inside.

Those tablets sat there absolutely stationary, staring at her, not a bit impatiently; they were in on the secret.

Her graying red hair frizzing out like a hallo around her face, she studied those tablets and the pink pen lying next to them with an extraordinary almost contemplative curiosity. Her hand sprung into motion and reached for that pink pen—what a lovely color—and clicked it on. The sharp intensity of that little click startled her; it seemed to take a moment for her to realize that her thumb had been a cause for that effect.

She smiled quite proud of her accomplishment. Then she looked over at that arrangement of tablets. The football player was just a little too much for her on this peaceful night. He might jostle Leonard awake. Mickey Mouse, Mickey Mouse, no, she was in a more meditative mood.

There was the lady slipper growing there quite contentedly, perhaps too contentedly. Finally, she looked at that spooky earth, like some huge eye it stared at her in unblinking observation—yes, the perfect tablet on which to start.

Dressed in purple, elephants parading across her shoulders, she placed the tablet on her lap. While the night nestled around her, she sat in that yellow-lit room. Her fingers pried open that stiff cardboard cover with the celestial photograph and turned it on the metal spiral binding—another physical revelation to reveal a blank sheet of paper.

At first, the blankness seemed so daunting. It was like a big doorway into nothing, some obscuring snowstorm. How could she ever step into a place that she had never dreamed of before? For an instant, her body froze—all that absolute possibility in front of her, no rules to bend or men to tease and cajole. She took a deep breath, put her pen to that sheet, and dove in.

October 15, 1996

Well, I suppose all I have to do is keep writing. If I keep writing, the page will fill up, and I will have written.

Am I making sense yet? Does writing mean that I have to make sense?

When I think of making sense, I think of Leonard, but I don't want to think of Leonard tonight. That's why I hate writing.

Writing is supposed to make sense, and sense seems to be beyond me. I don't know how people actually tie things together in some kind of order.

When I read whatever I have written, I sound either like an absolute idiot or, even worse, a phony.

I like to keep people guessing. I love the mystery of postcards.

Talking about being an idiot, why do I feel so stupid around Leonard so much of the time? I hear him snoring in the other room now. I like him better when he sleeps. He's there all warm and innocent and very simple.

When he really sleeps soundly, he's like a plant. His breathing is barely interrupted when I come back to bed, but his whole body moves toward me like it's reaching for the light. Of course, if I've happened to be out with a friend that night or even had too long a conversation on the phone, he never sleeps soundly.

When I crawl into bed, he lays there frozen in his bed. Like a rock, he doesn't even need to breathe.

The bed feels cold. If I don't say anything, he'll lay there comatose except that every few minutes, his whole body will convulse into an exasperated breath that releases rough as slow scraping sandpaper, the kind of breath that demands some kind of remark.

So I say something like "How are you, honey?"

I used to really want to know. Now I don't so much anymore because a question seems to be a kind of signal to him that he can scold me, and he has a special way of scolding. He takes a tortured breath and shudders as he turns to me into the night.

Even in the dark, I know what his face is like—a spooky stone mask, but his eyes burn. His words shoot out small and hard in my direction. His face is always the same when he's like that. "How could you be so late?" or "How could you talk on the phone so long?" or "Why do your friends only want to talk with you? Don't they know that you're living with me?"

I never know really what to say. If I say, "Oh, honey, I'm so sorry that I upset you," he goes into a long catalogue of all sorts of things that I didn't know I was doing. If I reassure him, "Oh, honey, I'm so glad to see you. I love you so very much. You're so important to me," he keeps asking me more questions like "How could you spend all that time with someone else if you loved me?" If I try to make some kind of excuse, then I'm really in trouble. "It's only ten p.m., honey. I tried to be real quiet, but I have a life too."

For a moment, his face hardens even more. He shuts those burning eyes of his as if he has to seal up all apertures to really build a head of steam. And I can tell that pressure is building up inside. I stop breathing too.

And I just know that I have done something wrong. And I probably have.

I know that I am careless. Besides, if I don't admit it, he starts cross-examining me, trying to persuade the jury, but the jury already knows that Leonard is right.

Everyone knows he's right. Besides, the sooner I break down, the sooner the trial ends, and then he becomes merciful and only sentences me to keep a little closer to him.

By this time, his body's warm again, and he is reaching for me like a child who only wants to be loved. I make some little promise and then comfort him. Somewhere in the tears and embrace, I feel some need burning inside him that only I can satisfy.

Now he's on top of me looking at me so tenderly, pleading, while his body starts pushing into me. There he's inside now. I feel his large cock inside me, and I know that everything is all right.

It's just that he loves me so much, and I need to try a little harder.

Then my own body starts moving in his rhythm. For just a moment, I think of things far away and long ago anywhere outside the room.

Then I notice his face hardening a little, and I try to come back to him. I let go into his need and I become his alone. He is thrusting so fast now that he is lost inside me, and I hold him so that he can find his way.

There there, he's coming now. I feel that final fury and the throbbing of his cock. I wrap him up in my love as he empties; he'll be safe now, my Len. After all, I love him, and that's the least that I can do.

He didn't seem to mind too much when I told him about the tablets, and writing doesn't seem as hard as I thought. I suppose I'll go back to bed now.

CHAPTER 15

IN PREPARATION FOR her trip, Frannie spent two whole evenings sorting through those piles of things that she called her life. Yes, she'll need this. She folded the shawl and placed it in the huge suitcase. No, she looked at the Betty Boop doll with regret and relief, consigning it to boxes of memories that she would leave at Leonard's.

She never had actually looked at all those items so carefully. Even when she moved, she had simply divided her possessions like some angel of judgment.

To one group, she nodded and pushed everything into a box marked "To Leonard's." Then she shook her head and sentenced everything in another very similar pile to the clutches of strangers or even to the fires of the city dump.

Even with her new resource of more careful discretion, she still awoke startled on that gray early morning of the first day of her honeymoon. Leonard had been up for two hours, already crossing off the last items on his list of preparations. A more confused Frannie slipped her nightgown off and uttered an "Oh my."

Wanda was generous enough to give the couple a ride to the airport. During the trip, periodically, Leonard would repeat to Frannie, "Wanda thinks of everything." Other times, he would turn to this paragon almost timidly (Frannie was riding in the back seat). "Wanda, you think of everything!"

Frannie, who didn't think of everything, was busy going over mental lists. Yes, she had her ticket; her passport; her toothbrush; the St. Christopher metal that Dodo gave her; plenty of underwear and a few bras—she was always so small, you know, but Leonard said that he liked her that way—money, although Leonard was so generous; and finally, her tablets for writing that already were beginning to fill up.

Yes, she was all ready. She too had thought of everything—at least she hoped she did.

Pens! That's what she forgot. She would have to get a pen, then she could write on the plane.

She gathered up the tools of her charm, and just as Leonard was once again saying, "Wanda you remember everything!" Frannie caressed his shoulder from behind and said, "Oh, Leonard, you know I just realized that I didn't bring anything to write with. You know how I forget things sometimes." She tried to look endearing.

Leonard and Wanda glanced at each other. Wanda was in a crisp blue suit, and her hair was as brisk and perfect as a computer chip.

Just in the last month though, she had started using a jasmine scent. Leonard smiled apologetically at her and turned around to Frannie with a smile that was just a little admonishing. "What did I tell you about keeping lists, Frannie? That way, you don't have to trouble your head with all kinds of information and then still forget something."

"Oh, Leonard, what would I do without you." She continued to caress his shoulder urgently.

Perhaps it was the tension of the trip, but his body instead of softening seemed to become tauter under her ministrations. Without turning around, he said, "I've got an extra in my briefcase."

Frannie settled back into her seat reassured; Wanda and Leonard sat in silent communion up front.

Finally, he said to no one in particular, "Wanda remembers everything!"

Wanda smiled a very composed smile and continued to smell of jasmine.

On the plane to New York, Frannie reminded Leonard about the pen. Somewhere over Indiana, she made the first entry of the trip.

October 20, 1996

What a surprise.

When we got to the airport, who should I see waiting for us at our gate: Dodo, I mean, Dwayne, of course. Leonard didn't look completely pleased, but you know how Leonard hates surprises. It was amazing.

As Leonard and I were rushing to our gate, we weren't late of course. Leonard always has to get to places ahead of time. I looked down the airport corridor, and I saw Dodo's bouncing silhouette. He walked on the balls of his feet. I had no idea that he would come to see us off. Something in me kind of caught, and I wanted to cry.

We all came together, and Dodo put his arm around me like it was he and I who were headed out on the trip. And then Dodo actually hugged Leonard. I had never seen anyone hug Leonard before.

After the first shock, he actually smiled. Then all cozy, we walked to a McDonald's to get coffee.

Dodo glanced at me, sad and protective, while Leonard was describing our (what's the word? *Agenda*? No...) itinerary in exhausting detail.

Then out of the clear blue, Dodo said, "I'm real glad that you two will have a chance to do this." He was smiling, but his eyes seemed a little sad.

This would be the first time in many years that he and I won't be around to meet for coffee.

Then all three of us sat down at our gate just as a voice over the speaker said that boarding was beginning.

When our rows were called off, Leonard shot to the line. For a moment, I felt torn between the two men. I hugged Dodo again and quickly ran to follow Leonard's lead, but midway between them, I turned to Dodo and hollered, "I love you, Dodo."

Dodo saluted me, and in a quieter voice but still loud enough for me to hear, he said, "I love you too, DeeDee."

Oh, I hate having to put things in sentences. To me, it seems that things are kind of strung together like pearls, and sometimes the string breaks, and all the pearls scatter in every which way. With a sentence, I had to finish one idea off before I got started on the next. Oh well.

As usual, I was terrified of flying. I always felt like the plane was going to explode, and I was going to be hurdled out into the sky, screaming.

Leonard was very patient with me. He kept patting me on the leg. He really does love me, and knowing Leonard, if the plane exploded, he would find some way to save us. Who knows what he could figure out in those last terrifying moments; my Leonard is very resourceful.

They had a four-hour stopover in New York.

Jostling through the airport, Leonard marched in resolute lead. Though normally she had a meandering, wondering style of walking, to keep up with Leonard, she had learned to bend forward slightly with shoulders up and head trailing ever so slightly behind as she was pulled along in his wake.

He found the correct gate for their departure and silently sat down on an orange plastic chair; Frannie followed suit. Immediately, he pulled out his briefcase, snapping it open (she watched him sort through it), and then pull out a very thin black box barely deep enough to hold a single tablet.

He flipped it open; it was a computer. He touched a button, and the screen sparkled on. Even before she could say that she needed to look for a bathroom, his fingers were playing over the keys as he stared at the screen with eager intensity. He nodded vaguely in her direction. "Sure, honey, you go ahead. I need to review some cases."

She tried to make eye contact. "Are you sure? I can't get you some little old thing."

He looked up at her, puzzled for a moment. "No, you go ahead. I'm busy."

She left that orbit of his resourcefulness, banished to her own more idiosyncratic choices.

Once she was beyond the reach of his eyes, she perked up to her surroundings and noticed how people in New York seemed shorter. Unlike the airport in Minneapolis where people kind of waltz along, here people were rushing past each other with great urgency.

She dodged her way to the rest room. Women filed in out of those bathroom stalls at record speed. For the life of her, she had never seen women finish so quickly.

On the way back to her seat, still basking in the relief of an emptied bladder, she noticed a small boy being ushered to a seat very close to where Leonard's form was hunched over his computer. The little boy had a baseball cap on backward, a green sweat suit with "Green Bay Packers" scrawled across it, and two armfuls of toys that seemed to be sticking out in every direction.

As soon as the stewardess sat him down, he dumped everything down on the floor and began taking apart some sort of ray gun.

Frannie loved clutter; she sat between the boy and Leonard. She looked at the boy tentatively; it was hard to tell if she simply wanted to join in the fun or if she felt some maternal concern for a lone child on a journey.

Finally, she patted him on the shoulder and fixed her eyes on him with her most sympathetic look. He glanced in her general direction for a split second and then proceeded in his dismantling of the gun.

There she was sandwiched between two males who were both too engrossed in their games to notice the airport, let alone her.

Very casually she tried talking to Leonard first, "You know, my dear, you were right. I never should have worn my new shoes for the trip. I'm getting blisters on my heels."

Leonard looked up. "I told you not to wear new shoes for the trip. Why don't you change into your old shoes, Frannie? I'm sure you will be more comfortable. We have some walking to do today."

Frannie, for her part, seemed absolutely intrigued by her shoe dilemma, especially since she finally had his attention. "What a good idea, although my old shoes are packed in my suitcase and Lord knows where that is right now." She smiled at him in enthusiastic exasperation.

The computer was drawing him back like some siren. "I guess you'll just have to wait until we get to Rome. You can change shoes there." His gaze was locked onto the computer again.

But Frannie wasn't finished yet. "What I could do, I suppose, is to get some tissue and make little pads for my heels. Do you think that would work, Leonard?"

"Hmm."

She stared out the window into the setting sun for a moment and then quite matter-of-factly turned to the boy on the other side of her. "When I was a child, I used to have to play with dolls. That gun you're playing with looks much more interesting."

The little boy dropped it on his lap and picked up a computerized football game and frantically began pressing buttons.

Frannie could be determined too. She riveted her attention on the tiny footballers swarming across the screen like ants. "Oh, I see, it's like a football game. Those little squiggly things are the players, and you move the ball around with that little button. How clever!"

He didn't look up, but as his fingers punched at the buttons, a small voice issued forth. "*Those* are the Green Bay Packers. I'm from Milwaukee. My father says that the Packers are the best team in the world. The other team is the Baltimore Colts, but the Packers are going to win." His fingers scrambled on the buttons, and the squiggly figures rushed at each other. "There. There you go…touchdown! The Green Bay Packers win the Super Bowl again."

Frannie clapped in excitement.

Her excitement must have impressed him. "Do you want to play with me? You can be the Minnesota Vikings. They're a pretty good team. Not as good as the Packers."

"I was never very good at football, being a girl and all, but I'll try to give you a run for your money."

His momentary flash of interest seemed to suddenly fade. "My dad said that I shouldn't talk to anyone in the airport. The stewardess is going to take care of me." He glanced up at Frannie and recognized disappointment when he saw it. "Well, I suppose since you're a woman, I can talk with you." He took his hat off with automatic gentility.

For her part, Frannie relaxed into confidentiality. "I've always wanted to visit Milwaukee."

The boy was impressed. "I actually live in Milwaukee *and* Rome. My mom lives in Rome, and I am going to visit her for a while. My dad's new wife says that Rome would be a good place for me to go to school. She's having a baby."

"Well, I've always wanted a little brother."

"You can call me Brendan, but my friends call me Dan."

"My name's Frannie, but you can call me DeeDee."

"That's a funny name."

"I'm a funny girl."

"You're no girl. You're old."

Frannie turned her head away from her new charge for a moment and glanced at Leonard to make sure he was still absorbed in his game. She turned back. "I suppose so. I still like to play games."

Brendan nodded as he struggled to score another point for his Milwaukee Braves.

The stewardess, with hair puffed up like a yellow mushroom, approached from behind the two and placed her hand on his shoulder. "It's time for you to board now, Brendan." She couldn't help but notice that pile of toys and gadgets littering the floor around him. She salvaged a smile. "I'll just help you with these." She began ferociously pushing the toys into a pile while Brendan scored six more points. She glanced up at Frannie who seemed more interested in the touchdown than the stewardess's important task. "I see you have found a friend. Come with me now." The stewardess bent down and swept the toys into her arms, and as she stood up, somehow snagged Brendan's arm, and led him away toward the gate, their reluctant progress was suddenly stalled.

"I forgot my Milwaukee Braves hat—the hat my dad gave me." He twisted out of her grasp and ran back to the seat next to Frannie; sure enough on the floor leaning against a leg rested the hat.

He scooped it up in a flash, putting it on his head. He paused for a moment and then turned it around backward. In a loud child's whisper, he said to his new friend, "Maybe she'll bring you on next. You can bring your friend with the computer too if he wants to come along."

DeeDee smiled. "I'll be along soon."

Roaring up into the skies in the belly of the beast, those first terrifying minutes seemed to be eased for Frannie. After all, she had her two men to take care of now.

Dan was sitting two rows behind her. Both Dan and Leonard couldn't use their electronic gadgets while the plane took off; they needed her.

Frannie was at her most charming, making conversation with Leonard and regularly turning around to give little waves of reassurance to Dan.

She hardly noticed that her own fear until the plane leveled off, and her two friends once again became absorbed in their appliances. If only she had remembered to bring a book. As for writing, if God had intended people to write while flying, he would have created them with wings and a free hand. At least that's what she said to Leonard.

Despite her disclaimer, once again, she began writing.

Somewhere over the mid-Atlantic, she fell asleep. When she woke, that shortest night of her life was ending in a pale pink glow in the east, and she could just make out the opaque edge of land between the sky and the sea.

Only when the plane began a gradual shuddering descent and once again, her two friends were signaled to turn off all electrical appliances, did she take up her responsibility for her two charges.

She kept waving at Dan until the stewardess came by to ask if she was all right.

Even though everyone on board was cautioned to stay seated until the plane had completed stopped, when the wheels of the craft touched down and the momentum diminished to the speed of a slow taxi, people unclicked their seat belts and in unison stood up to begin scrambling to reach into the overhead compartments to desperately gather their possessions as if the end of the world was at hand.

Leonard was leading the charge to safety with Frannie in tow. As she was rushed down the aisle, she made an apologetic wave to Dan. He was very still, his face almost a mask as he sat shipwrecked among his toys. "Dan, I'll wait for you outside."

He straightened his hat and turned on his football game.

She caught up with Leonard. The stewardesses and pilot lined up in a gauntlet at the exit of the plane.

"I hope you had a comfortable trip. Thank you for flying United. I hope you enjoy your stay. Goodbye now. We hope to serve you again."

The crowd oblivious to the crew's blessing raced out of the plane and into a long covered gangplank of a tube. When they stepped out, they were in Italy.

"Leonard, stop! We need to wait for a minute. I want to see if that dear little boy is all right."

Leonard seemed absolutely baffled by his arrested progress. "What little boy?"

"You know, Brendan, the little boy who sat by us in the airport."

He stared at Frannie as if she was a stranger whose face he was trying to recall. There that's it, he had it now.

She tried to look charming.

"Okay, Frannie, but we can't stay long. We have a train to catch to Rome."

"It'll just be a minute, just a minute." Though her voice was pleading, she stationed herself in the gate as immobile as the Rock of Gibraltar.

For Leonard's part, he studied the train schedule with the concentration of a court brief.

The herd coming out of that passageway began thinning. Old ladies and parents with children were now trickling out, and there was Dan with the brisk blond stewardess.

The two stepped from the tube into the airport. DeeDee waved both her arms at him to get his attention, but his eyes passed over everybody. He was searching for something. He broke away from the stewardess, abandoning her to his paraphernalia and rushed into the crowd. A slim dark-haired woman opened her arms, and Brendan rushed in.

Frannie was left with both her arms waving in the air.

"So he's okay, Frannie. He's found his mother. We have to go." Perhaps Leonard noticed the empty look on her face; he paused. "That was very kind of you to take care of that little boy."

She smiled and tried to twinkle at her husband.

That was his signal. Like an icebreaker, he led the way through those excited gesturing people who clustered together and spoke a language that she didn't understand. She followed in his wake submerged in the phrases and commotion of Italy, staying very close to her Leonard.

CHAPTER 16

October 21, 1996, Rome

Leonard is already calling it Roma. Of course, he has been listening to Italian language tapes for months.

I was never very good with languages. Even though both of us barely slept on the plane, we were so excited that we only took a very short nap in our hotel room, and by midafternoon, we were out walking the streets of Roma.

We walked for five hours. I'm glad that I was wearing my comfortable shoes again.

The wadded toilet paper didn't work very well. Every once in a while, I would see a little boy who reminded me of Dan, but when I looked closer, it was never him.

I hardly remember anything that I saw, just little cars speeding around beeping their horns. If it wasn't for Leonard, I don't think I would have made it across a single street.

Cars seemed to come out of nowhere. I'm surprised the streets aren't littered with corpses.

At street corners, Leonard would look even more determined than usual, and then as if he didn't have a fear in the world, he would simply start stepping across the street. Like magic cars would stop, although occasionally, he would have to give some impatient driver a fierce glare.

The buildings all seemed pushed up to the street hardly leaving room for sidewalks. The sun was still up when we started walking, and all the buildings looked golden and romantic, but as the sun went down, everything turned a murky gray.

I never saw so many pillars in my life. At a certain point, lights went on in the city, floodlights shining on those huge old buildings. Against the darkness, each building looked like some memory from a long time ago. The cars stopped rushing around as much.

Suddenly, from out of the shadows came people walking arm and arm up the narrow streets into broad courtyards. Leonard said that they were called piazzas. Double *z* sounds like "its." So that's why we say pizza the way we do.

The whole city became one meandering, murmuring evening parade. I guess it was more like a procession than a parade.

People seemed so peaceful. Either they would be walking arm in arm, or they would be casually touching each other's shoulders or arms for emphasis. All the time, they would be gesturing and talking with quiet excitement. As if that wasn't enough they would very warmly nod at people passing by them.

At first, I thought that they were only nodding at people they knew, but people even nodded at Leonard and me as we sped past them.

People had such lovely shoes here, and even though they dressed kind of formally, they seemed real friendly. It's like in the evening people have nothing better to do than stroll in the dusk and say hello to each other.

I saw so many mothers and daughters walking around, whispering, and nodding; eyes and hands and faces and whole bodies gesturing and leaning into each other. It almost made me miss my mother, although she had been dead for so long.

I can't imagine us ever leaning into each other intimately. She was always so small and perfect; she walked around with a smile that seemed to alert the world that only she, of all mortals, really understood perfection.

I was too tall, my hips were too big, and my hair were too unruly and red. No matter how hard I tried, I always seemed to be stumbling into things. I could still hear her say, "Now, Frannie, is that how a young lady acts?"

When I grew older, she didn't even have to say it anymore; she could just smile in that disappointed superior way of hers.

I don't know why I'm thinking of this all of a sudden. Here I am simply writing about Rome, and my mother barges in completely uninvited back to Rome.

Leonard had a map and led us to a park with sidewalks winding through it. All along the paths, I saw shadowy stone busts staring at us. I know in American cities, it is always a little dangerous to walk in parks at night, but it is different here; people just keep strolling in the evening as fearless as can be.

I stopped to look at a tree that I didn't recognize. I asked Leonard if he thought it was an olive tree. Italy is supposed to have a lot of olive trees. For once, he didn't have the answer.

From the darkness, I heard a woman's voice saying, "*Querci!*"

I squinted my eyes and saw a solid-looking middle-aged woman approaching us. She seemed formal but friendly. I said, "So this isn't an olive tree?"

She said, "*Querci* (or something that sounded like that)."

Leonard whispered in my ear, "That means oak tree."

She was close enough now so that we could make eye contact. She smiled at me like I was an old friend, and for a moment, I felt that I too was a part of this evening in Rome.

I noticed a small dog at her feet that suddenly scampered away from his distracted mistress.

She yelled out to the dog, "Salvatore!" loudly but just as dignified as can be.

The kind woman and I looked at each other for a single instant and both of us start laughing for no special reason. Then she ran off into the night looking for Salvatore. I felt a little guilty, she having lost track of her dog to tell me the name of the tree, but I loved the way we caught each other's eyes and just laughed.

Once again, Leonard began pointing out floodlit buildings, telling me their names. I reached for his hand. For a moment, he was silent. I thought I felt him smile. Then he went on with his catalogue. His voice mixed in with the night sounds and smells of Rome.

Oh yes, there is one little problem.

Before we lived together, when we had sex once and a while it seemed fine, but now, well, I just don't know what to do about it.

As ordinary fare, I may not really like sex. The smells you know.

A few weeks ago, I asked Leonard to brush his teeth first before we made love. When he would stick his tongue in my mouth, I would taste every little thing that he had eaten in the previous meal. After that, my Leonard very gallantly brushed his teeth whenever he wanted to make love. It had become a signal for me to get ready.

Then that taken care of, I started having difficulty with the smell of his underarms if we made love at the end of the day. I felt like such a baby. I know I am so silly about these things. How does Leonard put up with me?

I know how much sex means to him. To make a long story short, I asked him to shower first. So now he brushes his teeth and showers hardly muttering at all.

It is better, maybe even a little romantic to see how this big grown man who other men seem afraid of, sprucing up on his hygiene just for me.

THE TWO SLEPT that night in their room in the pensione—home sweet home.

He had a way of wrestling and grimacing in the trap of sleep until some internal alarm bell seemed to go off releasing him to the new day.

This morning, his eyes flashed open, but he continued taking deep rapid gasps of air, heart pumping in his ears. He stared out, terrified for several moments before his dream released him. As his very private own morning dawned on him, his breaths slowed down in relief.

There was a brief moment where he almost looked relaxed. Then he noticed the dim light sneaking through the shutters of the window. As the light got brighter and strange voices filtered up from the street, his breath again began becoming rapid as he vigilantly glanced from side to side of the room, reconnoitering the onslaught of day. When his eyes shot over to Frannie, they narrowed, and his hands clenched in some particular determination. For just the briefest of moments, his shadowy face hardened into a mask of cold reproach until something softer, some warm reassurance filtered through.

Then he seemed to notice almost accidentally how the now bright Roman morning outside was casting brilliant thin streaks of light through the shutters and onto Frannie; he bent over and kissed the delicate hand that gently rose and fell on her abdomen.

So much of Italy happenings in the street. He slipped his clothes on, his belt tinkling in the striped gloom. He clicked on the little lamp on his side of the bed. Crouching in that bright dome, he began studying his map and making plans for the day. His consort turned onto her side, away from him, without waking.

When he could contain his resolve no longer, he clicked off the light and walked over to the windows. His hands fumbled with the latch for a second, and then suddenly, the room was filled with the sunny Roman morning. He looked out, took a deep slow breath of the warm air, and smiled; a day of Roman adventure ahead, and Frannie was with him. He walked to the bed, crawling over the crackling maps, bent down, and kissed Frannie's ear.

That exposed hand of hers quivered. Her eyes remained closed, but her lips muttered "Hmm" midway between a sigh of pleasure and a moan.

"Frannie, honey, we're in Rome. It's time to get up. You don't want to miss breakfast. I've marked the map. We have to see so many things today before we catch the train to Lecce."

She squinted her eyes open. "That's nice, dear." Her eyelids squeezed shut.

He started jumping up and down on the map-covered crackling bed.

"Okay, okay, I'll get up." She managed a smile.

"We'll start with the Santa Maria Maggiore, pass the Trevi Fountain, and skirt around the Palazzo Borghese. We'll end up at the Vatican just in time to head back to our room, pick up our suitcases, and catch the train."

She sat up on the edge of the bed. "My, you've been busy this morning."

His earnest Boy Scout face darkened in controlled complaint. "We're in Roma, Frannie. We don't want to waste time, do we? We have things to do!"

She looked at the maps scattered on the bed and out the opened window; her eyes finally settled on his face. With a strained voice and a smile, she said, "You know, Leonard, you're really wonderful. You take such good care of me, don't you?" She looked into his complaining eyes and twinkled.

As if that smile was contagious, the corners of his mouth began tilting up. "We've got so much to see, Frannie. We have to."

One-half hour later, Leonard ushered Frannie out of the room and down a tight corridor lined with old posters of Italy and grateful letters sent from people all over the United States.

The couple passed by the main desk now abandoned to a large bouquet of plastic flowers. They followed the smell of coffee into a small room with red wallpaper and a large crystal chandelier that hung dangerous low over four shiny round black tables. Each table had four empty chrome chairs around it.

Leonard and Frannie sat down at the window table. A thin middle-aged man with a severe black-and-white tuxedo approached their table with the formality of a priest approaching an altar. Perhaps it was the dignity of his job, or then again, it might simply have been some slight difficulty with the language, but he spoke in deep, very measured tones marked with an ominous cadence and mysterious pauses. "Good *morn*-ing. I hope *that*...you had *a*...comfor-*ta*-ble... rest. Would you *like...cof*-fee...this morning...*yes?*"

Leonard and the waiter looked at each other with competing severity. Frannie broke the standoff. "Oh, what a *love*-ly room...for *breakfast*. We...would *love* some...coffee. I have...*heard* that *Italian* cof...fee is...*won*-derful." She seemed not only to have been infected by the cadence of his language but had also turned up her volume to increase the rapport. "*We*"—she proudly pointed to herself and Leonard—"are from…*the* United *States*."

The waiter bowed to the signora.

Leonard stared at the waiter tapping his finger on the table. The waiter turned abruptly from Leonard and mysteriously disappeared through the swinging black door.

That swinging door seemed to seal the couple off from any opportunity for breakfast. A loud conversation was taking place between the dignified waiter and an excited woman somewhere behind the black door.

Pans were clanking in a sink. Then a loud hissing sound of an espresso machine silenced the voices.

Frannie nodded knowingly to Leonard.

The door swung open again.

The slightly offended waiter glided to the table. "Signora." He carefully placed a cup down at Frannie's place and smiled with a little sense of accomplishment. "Signor." He placed another cup, a little too definitely in front of Leonard.

Both cups were topped with frothy milk and a little sprinkle of what smelled like nutmeg.

The waiter turned around with a little jerk and disappeared behind the swinging door where once again the two yelling voices and many clattering plates seemed to ricochet off the kitchen walls.

The door swung open again, and once again, silence ensued. With the composure of an iceberg, the waiter placed a plate of bread, a cool rectangle of butter, and a pot of very red strawberry jam in the center of the table.

Leonard grabbed a piece of bread and asked for another cup of coffee.

The waiter looked at him stunned. "Ano-*ther*…cup…of…*coffee?*" He turned wounded eyes onto Frannie as if surely she must understand the affront of this request.

She simply said, "Oh my."

Leonard had that fierce look on his face that he reserved for crossing streets. "Coffee. I'd like another cup of coffee!"

The waiter looked at Leonard with cool contempt. "*Si*" and clipped back into the kitchen.

As the espresso machine was hissing again, Frannie could hear the waiter yelling. When the kitchen door pushed open, the waiter looked at neither American as he slammed the rattling cup and saucer in front of Leonard. This time, there was no foam or nutmeg on top of the coffee.

Leonard ignored the waiter too and grabbed a piece of bread and splayed butter on it with ferocious strokes.

The waiter retreated with his honor intact.

Frannie stared out the window to the building across the shadowed courtyard where a woman in a red flowered housedress was bending out of a third-story window. She was hanging laundry out on a rope tied to the opposite wall. First, she would hang an article of wet clothing on the line. Then she would give the line a very calculated yank; the line was tied round a pulley. There would be a squeaking sound, the article of clothing would jerk out, and she would hang out another article of clothing. How wonderful!

Frannie returned her attention to the dining room and picked out a piece of bread. Touching the spongy soft center first, she brought it up to her nose. The smell of yeasty fresh bread mixed with the aromas of coffee and nutmeg and finally the funny slightly sour smell of a Roman morning all mixed inside her. She bit into the resistance of the hard crust, all brown and crackly, until her teeth slid into the promise of soft whiteness. She smiled at Leonard even without trying.

CHAPTER 17

October 22, 1996

We spent the morning walking around in Rome, squeezing in everything that we could. Leonard had a very strict itinerary.

This afternoon, we took the train and headed off to a place called Lecce. It was supposed to have a lot of old baroque buildings in it.

Leonard said he had a passion for the baroque—whatever that was, the baroque, I mean, not his passion. I know his passion well.

This morning, we saw Roman piazzas and fountains and so many statues. For a quick lunch, we stopped at a shop crowded with beautifully dressed and well-shod Romans.

All of them were busy, gesturing and talking loudly, but still, they were very polite in a kind of old fashioned way.

Even though everyone was eating while either romancing or scolding someone, they seemed to have an almost mystical sense of where things are in space.

In the midst of all that commotion, I opened my purse to get some money; I was treating Leonard.

My address book must have fallen out. A middle-aged man, busy eating and very excitedly talking to a young woman, bent down; without interrupting his lunch and conversation; bowed to me with the address book in hand; and smiled this little smile, like I was a dear but naughty child. Leonard said that I needed to be more careful. I supposed he's right, although I loved meeting that man.

Then we caught the train to Lecce. A thin young man with reddish gold hair entered our compartment and asked if he could sit with us. He was very pleasant-looking and spoke wonderful English. He said that he was from Denmark, and that his name was Allen. Of course, I said yes.

Although right after I said it, I realized that I should have asked Leonard first. Leonard didn't like people to come too near him unless he invited them. He proceeded to ignore us for forty-five minutes.

Allen and I had a wonderful conversation about Anne Rice and world peace. He was only twenty-two and was en route to Bosnia on a peacekeeping mission for the United Nations. I forget how close all these countries were to each other. I suppose if I were twenty years younger, I would have fallen in love with him—such a sensitive and adventurous young male.

As the dry hills south of Rome passed by our window, I found him dear and humane and a little naive. Maybe I'm naive too because we ended out talking about all the things that confused us and that spacey feeling when things didn't really make sense.

Eventually, Leonard turned away from the window and started talking with us, but the conversation changed after that.

Both Leonard and Allen began gradually raising their voices and talking about facts. It really wasn't fun anymore. By the time Allen departed at Bari, I was glad that he was leaving. Leonard got so upset you know.

We got into Lecce at 10:00 p.m., and it seemed like a spooky ghost town except for those fast little cars with lights shining that keep beeping their horns. Even so, Leonard wanted to look at the city.

After we pulled our suitcases a couple of blocks (thank god for suitcases with wheels), he found a funny old hotel with tiny rooms and with old-fashioned beds. Leonard seemed so proud of his find; he was so economical. Then we walked on narrow sidewalks through narrow old streets lined by large crumbling fancy shoe shops. I must sound like I'm obsessed with shoes, but I never saw so many shoe shops before in my life and such nice ones.

By the next afternoon, I could not stand seeing one more "exquisite example of the baroque."

While Leonard went off to see more monuments, I parked myself in a large piazza to watch the end of the afternoon. Leonard may have even been a little relieved to leave me behind; I tend to lag.

There were palm trees and what looked like rhododendrons and a large bronze statue of some military hero sitting on a horse. He had an expression on his face like Leonard, all stiff and determined. One hand was perched authoritatively on his hip, and the other was resting on his sword. I could almost hear him say, "Frannie, you need to be more careful."

A young couple sat opposite me on a bench. She wore sunglasses and looked very content. He had his arm around her; his hand was placed gently on her left breast, like it was holding a fragile bird, lightly but with great intent. I tried not to look too conspicuous as I watched them. Something about the secrecy of it all. I felt exquisitely invisible except for an occasional pigeon that would notice me and land near by long enough to realize that I didn't have any food for it.

Maybe it's the tension of the trip, but last night, my left eye burst a blood vessel. I had cramping stools and sore feet. To add insult to injury, there was an empty potato chip bag under the bench of the lovers. It's different than traveling with Dodo, but I suppose I was different too.

The girl on the bench opposite threw back her head languidly onto her boyfriend's shoulder. His hand seemed to press just a little more firmly on the fluttering bird.

Leonard and I moved on to place called Reggio tonight…that was if he comes back. How silly of me! Leonard always came back; he was the epitome of faithfulness.

The shade from the buildings finally submerged their bench, and the lovers left. They're gone now; I miss them.

Some birds up in the palm trees were making cackling sounds, complaining as a damp coolness takes over the park leaving that determined soldier at guard shining in the last of the sunlight. Yes, Leonard will be coming back.

I hope we find a place to settle down in soon. A slightly stiff walking young man with long hair clicked his shiny boots and turned in my direction as he walked by. I avoided his glance.

THE TWO HEADED south, like migrating birds, Leonard taking up the lead. Frannie trailed behind, sometimes dreamy other times with a tight concern pushing her eyebrows together so intensely that a wrinkle etched itself between them.

For the next two weeks, they seemed to stop almost every evening in one new town or another. Leonard would jump off the train; Frannie would push an immense suitcase into his waiting arms. More delicately she would step off the train and pull down her smaller suitcase. Then together they would head off looking for some hotel that would be sunny and old and quaint in some town that hopefully would embrace them and beg them, "Come stay."

Alas, what they found were hotels more expensive than Leonard had imagined and cities too busy to be curious about two middle-aged strangers who had come at the end of the tourist season. Perhaps Italians had enough of being gracious to visitors all summer.

Usually after dark, Leonard and his lady would trudge into some small hotel. Leonard took a pride in always getting a good deal. They never picked expensive-looking hotels. After all, they weren't simply tourists who didn't know better; Leonard always knew better.

He would start by facing the formal-looking hotel clerk and say, "Buona sera," with a kind of tight-lipped challenge.

The clerk would look up like the pope glancing at his audience. In very careful though not accurate Italian, Leonard would ask for a room for the night. The clerk would either answer in halting English or in Italian so fast-paced that Leonard would be left confused—a state to which he certainly was not accustomed.

And Frannie always knew when Leonard didn't like something. Her breathing would become shallow; the furrow between her eyebrows becoming deeper by the minute until some sort of arrangement would be made between Leonard and the world.

Finally, the couple would pull their suitcases through hallways that seemed to get narrower the further south they traveled in Italy. Ensconced in a tiny room with beds in which Garibaldi must have slept, they would slip into exhausted sleep even Leonard.

"Good night, Lenny," she would mumble from her side of the bed.

Leonard would be already slumped over on his side. "Good night, Frannie" would filter through the covers bundled around him.

Some nights, she would pat him gently on the bulge that was his hip. But always during the night, he would discover his resolve once again.

By morning, he would have vast stores of information and plans to share with his spouse.

Somewhere after Reggio, Frannie began calling him by the more diminutive title: Len. They had found their way all the way down to Syracuse in Sicily.

November 5, 1996

This morning, I woke up with a very mild pressure squeezing my temples.

Talking about temples, we had a full schedule today. My, how I wish he could let us relax. I feel so alone in this land of decaying palaces and dark streets with little cars squirming around like dangerous insects. Instead of buzzing, they beep menacingly.

Today we needed to get an early start; I wonder if Leonard runs his business this way. Everyone who works for him must be continuously out of breath.

I know I shouldn't complain; he takes such good care of me. I feel like my mother, always complaining. I never wanted to be like her, and here I am a real bitch princess.

Sicily, Sicily, Sicily. The train ride yesterday was almost beautiful, but before reaching Syracuse, we passed through an endless stretch of oil refineries. It was like some demon had taken over the land. This horrid, spoiled place was the gateway to what I had hoped would be our resting place. Even the weather changed when we passed through those miles of refineries. The sky turned a dank gray.

When we finally escaped from hell, the train entered this sort of ramshackle area where huge gray apartment buildings were mixed up with old sooty factories.

We were entering Syracuse. The train slowed down a little maybe so we could get a better look at a huge billboard with a voluptuous woman on it advertising some kind of candy—large breasts, large breasts.

The train inched its way through winding dark streets where children played while old ladies dressed in black, watched. I almost wished that we had gotten in town late at night, like we usually do, so that I could go right off to sleep.

We lugged our bags from the station. How does Leonard always know where to go?

We walked blocks through the ugly modern part of the city: barbershops, little factories, funny restaurants with old men in aprons standing in the doorway, shoe shops, apartments with laundry hanging over the streets, and cars, cars, cars. We crossed an old marble bridge from that dreary part of the city into a place just as crowded, but it looked more interesting, older, not by Italian standards I suppose. Old is at least two thousand years ago.

This city looked medieval, buildings huddled close and high, but in almost every corner, old churches or palaces would rise up straight from the street. Grimy carvings hung over doors and windows. A cool breeze from the nearby bay blew trash along the cobblestones.

Then I looked up ahead at an empty piazza. Huge broken columns rose up out of the ground—so huge that I swear only a fairy-tale giant could have erected them.

Stories of gods and ancient heroes flooded in. For a funny moment, I felt like I was experiencing thousands of years of stories, emperors, slaves, crusaders, princes; but all around the piazza, present-day Italians were baking bread and cutting hair and selling things in shops. I felt time all scrunched up. I'm getting carried away I know.

Leonard found a narrow old hotel that was on the edge of a piazza, the same piazza where I saw those huge broken columns sticking up.

I love the chaos of time here. We squeezed our bags into the skinny room. I wonder what I would do if I were here alone.

I had never traveled alone. Isn't that funny? People thought I had because of the postcards I had sent, but I was always with somebody. Maybe I hate to travel, but I hate being left at home even more.

My father was an officer in the air force. When he went off alone, I was left with my mother, and I don't even want to think about that.

Every time we moved to a new city and school, I felt out of place. I found that if I could tell marvelous stories about all the places where I had lived, I would sort of fit in.

My father was such a disappointment to mother. Even with all that traveling, he never became more than a captain.

He never could do anything right, and then he divorced her and married a beautician.

It was me and Mom then. She bought a funny little house on the edge of downtown, and I was the only left to be a disappointment. No more traveling, no more stories.

High school was a gray blur. I think I was invisible.

Then late one afternoon while I was watching television after school, the police came to the door. They said that she forgot to turn on her directional blinker. When she switched lanes, the signal must have been out of order; she didn't make mistakes, although with a two-ton truck slamming into you, I suppose it doesn't matter.

Suddenly, I was the tragic girl with the dead mother. I didn't even have to talk about it. I could just look at people and kind of slump down a little.

That's when I met Dodo. He was very popular in high school. All the girls thought he was cute.

One day during recess, he came up to me all very solemn. "I am very sorry to hear about your great loss." What kind of kid says something like that?

But I liked the words *great loss*. Something about me was larger than life.

I realized that I was not really all alone anymore because I had that starring role to play: a girl with a great loss; I was in the very center of it. Even if I wasn't so great, my loss was. I think Mom would have approved. I was finally doing something right.

As soon as we stowed our bags in the room, we set off to see more sights. We had seen modern Syracuse and then medieval Syracuse, and now we were to see ancient Greek Syracuse.

Even though the nights had started to become cool and damp, the days could be baking hot. I know that I usually love heat and light, but all the noise and the glare here were sometimes too much.

I had gotten blisters on my feet the first day of the trip. With the almost constant walking Leonard and I do, the blisters had never healed. Complain, complain, complain. I try to be a good sport. Maybe my mother did too.

I always thought that Italians had big families, but even here in Sicily, most parents looked like they only have two children, usually a boy and a girl. I wonder how they work that out in this Catholic country where everyone calls the pope papa. I won't digress anymore.

When we got to the outskirts of town, we walked along a sidewalk so narrow that it seemed to be disappearing into the road that had become a highway. We had to share the road with those ferocious little cars. I said a silent prayer to one of those Madonnas with a dagger through her heart that I had seen at Lecce.

The sidewalk appeared again, and we found ourselves in front of a gate where a man was selling tickets.

Right beside him were tables covered with all kinds of statues and little souvenirs, like the state fair. Did I mention that it was hot and bright like a July afternoon in Minnesota?

We stepped through the gates onto a gravelly road, maybe made of limestone like so many other things here including the hills.

For a moment, I felt totally engulfed in the glare of sunlight hitting limestone all around until I noticed skinny little cats peering out from the scrub around the road. They would fasten their eyes on us, walk a few steps alongside us before giving up in frustration only to be replaced by another set of eyes and paws.

Suddenly, we found ourselves on the edge of a large expanse dug out of the earth. The huge bowl gleamed as if it was lit up. I realized that we were standing on the edge of the Greek theater. At least that's what the wasp like woman with the heavy Italian accent was explaining to a group of Americans. Leonard said that they were English. I stand corrected.

Without even asking permission from Leonard, I just sat down high up in that theater and listened. The woman's voice buzzed in the hot afternoon, and I just didn't care about anything but being drowsy in that funny time warp that I had slipped into.

Her voice echoed through my ears. She pointed to the lowest spot in the circle and said that was the stage. In brittle fast-fire English with a hammer beat, she started to tell the story of the place.

She said something like this: "Now, gentleman and ladies, what you see down below is the stage of the Greek theater. Syracuse was a powerful Greek city. This was one of the largest theaters in the classical world. You can imagine productions of Oedipus Rex or Medea when all these seats were filled.

"Everything around you was once covered in marble, but in the Middle Ages, this was used as a quarry for building materials for Syracuse. Even the largest pillars were used to construct a wharf out in the bay.

"Where we are standing now are the seats for the audience. That section there at the farthest point is where the actors stood, reciting the lines of the comedy or tragedy. Between the audience and the actors stood the chorus, reciting, dancing, and explaining the drama.

"In 300 BC, the Romans laid siege to the city of Syracuse. They broke through the defenses designed by Archimedes and took the city by surprise, murdering Archimedes in his home. They turned the theater into an arena for gladiatorial spectacles. Let's move on."

It was amazing how the tour guide could simply rattle through all that tragedy and then move on as if anything that ever happened here was simply entertaining information for we tourists. Not that I can actually repeat what she said verbatim, but once I started trying to remember, the words came to me. Isn't that funny? What a funny place Italy is.

War and murder and destruction seem like entertaining hazards, and through it all, the business of the city returned to normal with street vendors and hungry cats and people building monuments that someone else would tear down.

The tour guide's heels clicked rapidly against the stone pathway as she moved on to describe another scene that most certainly would end in tragedy. The crowd of Englishmen followed her like a flock of sheep. I found myself just sitting there and listening and dreaming in that hot afternoon in Sicily. Besides, it felt so good to get off my feet.

I suddenly heard a slightly irritated voice from the present. "As long as we're sitting, Frannie, this would be a good time to have our lunch. I brought some bread and cheese and vino."

At first, I thought that *vino* was the name of some dark-haired Italian who Leonard had invited along, but he reached in his sack to reveal a bottle of wine, vino. I got it. If Leonard starts sinking into Italian, who will I have to talk to? Or maybe that would be good. Sometimes I could pretend not to hear him.

I glanced over at him. "How wonderful, my dear." Then I went back to looking at the stage. Maybe it was defiance, but it felt so good to be off my feet.

For some reason, I kept thinking about the theater. I always thought that theater was about players and an audience. I always wanted to be one of the players; they get all the attention.

Greek theater sounds like it was a little different. There was that funny chorus standing between the audience and the players, explaining things all the time or adding emphasis or even just being a busybody.

The actors really didn't know what was going on. They were doomed to repeat the tragic or comic action the same way every night. Only the chorus really understands.

The audience has a double task. They are there to be entertained by the story. Thanks to the chorus, the audience was also there to learn something.

I don't know why this was so interesting to me or even if it's an accurate picture of Greek theater, but it just made me think. What if there really is in life some intermediary position between my fans waiting to be entertained by my latest story and me, the actor? Where is the chorus who stands between me and the audience and explains what this whole thing is about?

Maybe that's why I fell in love with Leonard. Somehow no matter where he was, he seemed like he knew what was happening and was willing, perhaps too willing, to enlighten me.

The sun must be making me dizzy. I looked over and noticed that Leonard had very precisely poured two paper cups of wine and cut two pieces of bread and two pieces of cheese. He did things so well as if he had memorized the script to perfection.

Sometimes I think he might need a chorus to explain things to him…really. I felt like I'm unfair to him, but I did want to shake him sometimes and tell him to stop. He didn't have to be right all the time. But who was I to say? I couldn't even find a hotel.

Sometimes I think what we had in common was that neither of us had a clue what was going on. I wonder if something was missing. I shouldn't think like that; everyone knew how fanciful I am, especially Leonard.

"Here's your wine, Frannie."

"You think of everything, Leonard."

I felt the bright afternoon sun and the cool cup in my hand.

"Are you all right? You seem so far away."

"Oh, I was just thinking there's so much history, and history's mostly bad news at least eventually."

"Don't you think that's rather a grim view of things?" His face was hardening. "Is this your way of letting me know that things are not going well? Whatever I do is never enough, Frannie."

Where is the chorus when I need it?

I drank some wine. It calmed me. I turned to him and smiled my best smile. "Oh, my darling, you know how grateful I am."

He still looked a little offended for the rest of the afternoon, but when we got back to our room, I let him make love to me.

My oh my, I was becoming a regular reporter.

It was two weeks into their trip now and still no sign of any place that was just right.

The night before, they had slept in another narrow pensione and, in the morning, woke up to the usual fresh bread and the single cup of coffee. Leonard now never asked for a second cup.

They had set off again on the sidewalks of Syracuse for one of Leonard's little journeys of discovery. "You know, Lennie, if there is anything I like about Italy, it's the smell of coffee. It smells so much stronger here."

Leonard nodded his head a little too casually before pulling a map out of his back pocket. "We'll see the ruins, and of course, I thought we would walk through the old town, and then..." his voice seemed to fade off, leaving them both abandoned to the river of noise and commotion—voices yelling, children running, and smells... smells of fish sitting out in the sun, pizza still hot from the oven.

For once in his life, Leonard looked overwhelmed. No matter how hard he stared at the map, his senses were engulfed in chaos.

Frannie was more at home with floundering. She was one step behind and placed her hand on Lennie's shoulder and simply whispered, "Len?"

His body tightened like a wire pulled taut and then slowly began to loosen under the touch of Frannie's hand and the sound of his name.

"Now, Lennie, I don't want to see one more ruins, and just for a few hours, I don't want to have anybody try to run me over. In the park over there, there's a bunch of buses. Let's just grab one. I don't care where it's going, and I'll be off my feet. It'll go somewhere we don't expect."

"I guess if your feet hurt, Frannie, that would be a good idea. I will talk to the bus drivers so that we can find the best place to go."

"I'm sure you will, Leonard. While you do that, I'll sit right on that sunny bench over there." She let go of his arm and without waiting for a reply strolled over to the bench where she sat down, spread her legs, and closed her eyes.

Sounds filtered through her relief, children's voice calling to each other in the park, "Andrea," "Mariangela," and then the sound of steps running together, and two young voices talking one hundred miles an hour at the same time. They only stopped long enough to laugh.

It took several minutes for Leonard to find the right bus.

Finally, in broken English, one thin bus driver, with dark hair and a smile missing a couple of teeth, looked at Leonard as if he was a dear but annoying child and said, "Come…with me…to sea…*bella, bella mare!*"

Lennie scampered back to Frannie as excited as any Italian child. "I found a bus to the sea, Frannie. We'll spend the day by the sea. It'll be just right for you, you'll see. The bus driver said it was beautiful. Bella mare."

Frannie opened her eyes. "Bella mare!"

November 6, 1996

I am sleeping a little better, or at least I don't feel so dead in the morning.

I had a dream about Dodo last night. It was a terrible dream—the kind of dream that I wouldn't tell anybody.

I was sitting in a room on a large soft sofa, and my skirt was pulled up. My legs were spread wide, and my genitals were on view for the world to see. To make matters worse, I was in the midst of my period.

Dodo was there, looking at me shocked and embarrassed as if he knew that there was something terribly wrong with me that the world should never see. Just then Leonard and my mother entered the room leading a whole group of strangers. I woke terrified.

Last night, in the little pensione in Syracuse (It's funny how Leonard was always looking for a bargain no matter what the price), I woke in the middle of the night to see Leonard sitting up in bed, alert and watchful. "*Shh*, you can go back to sleep. It's still nighttime, Frannie."

I felt alarmed at first; he seemed all prickly and vigilant like he was guarding a foxhole that we were in, and any minute, the enemy could start creeping out of their trenches to bayonet us.

I said, "Leonard, are we all right?"

He cautiously looked into the shadows of the room, patted me lightly on the shoulder, and said, "You can sleep a little longer."

He looked so desperately reassuring. I was wide-awake by this time.

Even though he was so resourceful, I suddenly thought how lonely it must be for him to always be on guard.

I moved over next to him and put my arm around him. I could feel some of his tenseness go away, but I could also see that he kept his eyes open still watching the room. He must have fallen asleep eventually because at about five in the morning, I heard him crying out. For a moment, I wondered if I should wake him to end his anguish, but then I knew if I woke him, he would start all his plans for the day. You know how he just keeps going all day and doesn't stop. I thought maybe if I left him be, he could actually finish his dream and have a few moments of rest.

And that morning, we had a full agenda of ruins and markets to see. I wanted to go on a picnic. Somehow when I am around him, all I think about is what he wants to do. I think that I have always done that with men. Maybe that's why I have never gotten married or maybe it's just my small breasts.

I remember when I had my first period. No one had really ever warned me about what was going to happen. One day, my panties were full of blood. Of course, I thought I was dying.

I went to talk to my mother. "Mom, there's blood down there."

She looked disgusted and wouldn't even glance below my waist. The way she stared at me, I knew it wasn't a disease but some terrible thing that I had done.

She walked in her bedroom and returned with a box. "Go in the bathroom and use these." She didn't look so disgusted now, just disappointed, maybe sad.

Even after all these years, I can't imagine my mother as ever having had a period. To add insult to injury, even though I bled in revolting amounts every month, my breasts refused to grow.

My nickname in high school was Ironing Board. Even when they actually grew a little, it didn't matter anymore; I was the girl with no boobs. My mother, who seemed primly free of anything as contaminating as periods, had beautiful nice-sized breasts, not so big that people would notice too much but just big enough to be perfectly womanly. She looked at herself with such pleasure in the mirror. She was perfect; no blood, just boobs.

She always said that men put up with a lot more from a woman with nice-sized breasts, especially if she was young and knew how to smile.

I taught myself how to smile.

Actually it was my mother's idea. She used to look at me with a funny little look of disapproval and say, "Frannie, if you'd only smile, some of those boys might like you." Of course, she didn't actually add "even though you have small breasts." But I knew what she meant.

Well, Leonard and I were walking down one of those tight little Italian streets, still in Sicily; I wonder why Italians are so noisy. Leonard was reaching for his map, always an ominous sign. But this time, he seemed a little bewildered.

That's when I decided to mention something about a taking a bus. There were a bunch of buses parked nearby, and I just wanted to take one of them and go anywhere, just to sit down and be with a whole bunch of people even if they were speaking Italian. At least we would all be headed in the same direction together. Len and I seemed so all alone. The further we went, the more I felt it.

While I sat down and closed my eyes, he found a very nice bus for us to travel on. He really can be sweet, especially on those rare moments when he appeared to be at a loss. Why do I feel so tender when he is in trouble? He found us a bus that went to the sea—*mare, bella mare,* he called it.

The bus was full of people. Two very serious-looking young men sat in the seat in front of us. When they heard us talking in English they turned around and started speaking, "Good morning...mister and missus...how are you... today?" They looked so proud of themselves.

Leonard said, "*Bonjourno*," and some other phrase that I didn't understand.

They looked a little embarrassed. I wonder what Leonard actually said.

The two young men glanced at each other and with a little bit of a smile said, "You speak... Italian...good," and then both started talking very rapidly.

Leonard kept nodding his head as if he understood.

For a moment, he looked so dear like some little child sitting with adults who he didn't understand. He so much wanted to be one of them.

Finally, they relented and began speaking English. They seemed so proud of each phrase that they were able to get out.

It turned out that they were two brothers who worked in the city in a shoe factory, and they were both going out to the country to see their mother who they both insisted was the best cook in the world. They lapsed into Italian for a moment as they described how wonderful her cooking was.

Then a little embarrassed, they turned to me and say, "*Scusi*, you cook good...*deliciosa*?" They mistakenly took my silence as modesty and looked to Leonard for assurance. "Your wife... she cook good?"

Leonard and I both looked at each other, and for the first time in days, maybe weeks, we started laughing, and I couldn't stop.

All the while, the bus was turning through thin grubby streets crowded with people walking and selling fish and laughing and scolding each other. The bus was speeding through those narrow streets, barely squeezing through.

Like in some very complex dance, the people were coolly almost elegantly sidestepping the bus barreling down at them. Even the dogs seemed to understand the complicated steps.

Am I good cook?

Leonard regained his composure more quickly than I did, and the two serious young men started to look alarmed as if perhaps they had made some terribly clumsy mistake.

They both started to say, "Scusi, scusi," over and over again.

I turned around with my biggest smile and said, "I cook like shit." I almost said, "and my breasts are too small."

They looked at me absolutely too confused, muttering the words *shit* and *food*, and then Leonard, of all people, let out this cackle of laughter, and we all began laughing again, this time, so hard that I cried.

"I am a terrible cook." I was able to get out between gasps.

The two boys stopped laughing and looked at me very sympathetically as if I were a dyslexic paraplegic or something; actually a little like my mother used to look at me.

Two older women seated behind us in black dresses solemnly carrying two huge bags of groceries glanced at me with something that looked like disapproval, either that or they had heartburn.

When I turned in their direction, I realized that they were my age. I felt like I needed to say something to them, so I said, "I just don't like to cook. I never got a long with my mother." They turned away.

The morning had been hazy, but now as we finally slipped out of the maze of streets that surrounded Syracuse, I saw how impossibly green everything was.

The sun turned bright, and the sky a kind of aching blue. I just wanted to get off the bus and leave those men behind and not have to try to be something for someone else; the bus was so noisy, everybody talking about their mother's cooking.

After my father left, the only bright spot in mother's life was the invention of remote control for the television. I didn't even question back then why she would dress up so absolutely perfectly to sit in front of the television to watch the soaps. She looked like she was waiting for a date.

Back then she had a better chance than I did. Did I say that she had nice-sized breasts, womanly in fact? Funny how Leonard and I never talk about our parents as if we sprang out of the ground like mushrooms.

A few minutes later on the very outskirts of town, the bus stopped, and very gravely and sympathetically the two young men said, "Good...bye." I smiled back and nodded, trying to look as womanly as I could.

They stepped off the bus, where a very short woman in a very dark dress greeted them as if they had just come back from some war from which they had barely escaped with their lives. They continued to look very solemn as she hugged them. I think she was younger than I am.

The bus started up. I didn't look at Leonard. We were passing small white stucco houses with what seemed like big yards, but every square inch was covered with vegetable gardens and fruit trees all carefully contained in the small space.

Then there were no more houses, just green fields; it really didn't matter to me. Maybe all that talk about cooking and all those women my age with grown-up sons, they all seem to know what they're doing and how they fit in.

We stepped off the bus on to a road, and the bus driver pointed to the left and said, "Mare, bella mare," as if we couldn't see that it was the sea.

Leonard led the way. I started hoping that we would be able to catch a bus back. I don't know why I was worried; Leonard thinks of everything.

CHAPTER 18

It seemed no matter how they tried, Leonard and Frannie couldn't find the perfect place in which to stay. Every few days, they would end up entering some dank Italian seaside town at night; the autumn rains had started, and Frannie was looking more like a refugee each day.

Finally, they had gotten completely around the island of Sicily and landed at Taormina. They got into the station at 4:00 p.m. The Italian sun had burned through the clouds and now glinted on the bay. The Mediterranean was the turquoise color of swimming pool bottoms; Frannie could almost smell the chlorine.

Leonard had his hopes up. This was the town that sophisticated Englishman discovered at the turn of the century.

Taormina became a celebrated place for them to visit. They would enjoy the sun and the sea and sometimes take pictures of naked adolescent boys eager for extra lira.

The train depot was very art nouveau, designed with simple colors and elegant elongated figures of people all carefully spaced across the borders of the walls.

There was a kind of antiseptic quality to the figures so different from the voluptuous extravagance of Sicily's churches. In this station, everything was spare and tasteful, though as Leonard noted quite filthy.

Frannie was just grateful they were in town ready to settle before the damp chill of a Mediterranean evening started to seep into her bones. She felt so much better when she unpacked in the daylight.

They stepped out of that tasteful station that was in deplorable condition. Ever resourceful Leonard had ascertained that in the tourist season, a very dependable bus stopped at the station and drove up to the town that was perched up on a towering hill overlooking the station—a hill that had withstood sieges of Saracens but opened its arms to Englishman of exquisite taste and dubious desires.

Leonard stopped at the ticket seller's window and informed the severe and uniformed personage there, "Certainly your bus is still running to the town."

That very official looking man behind the barred station desk looked embarrassed, then affronted and then began shuffling through tickets.

Leonard took that as an affirmation, and he and his spouse walked to the side of the road, waiting for the bus. Occasionally one and then the other would look up that towering hill toward their destination and perhaps even final home…so close but yet so far.

Leonard stood stone-faced and still calculating odds; this would be another test for his resourcefulness.

Frannie looked far more restless one minute, looking to Leonard for reassurance and the next pacing anxiously. Finally, she sat down on her suitcase with a defeated sigh and let her mind wander to somewhere else, some other ring of interest.

How she loved to be somewhere else. Though her body was slumped on a suitcase outside of Taormina, her mind, her mind was waiting by a road with another man. It was Dodo.

She and Dodo were stuck with no ride outside of Gallup, New Mexico. They had been waiting for what seemed like days. It was probably only a couple of hours. He nudged her on this hot forgotten stretch of highway.

Another car had just buzzed by, not even pausing at their two outstretched arms and curved thumbs.

Dodo loved to hitchhike; he seemed to know no fear, especially when DeeDee was around. "You know, DeeDee, what we need is a gimmick. Those cars pass by, and they just think were two ordinary people. Are we ordinary people, DeeDee? Well, are we?"

DeeDee shook her head, not all together convinced.

That was enough for Dodo. "Little do they realize that we, Hop Sun Fu, that's me, of course, and you, Me Ling Han, are genuine members of the Peking Opera."

Dodo had a very active imagination, and DeeDee was ready to go accompany it just about anywhere. In fact, prior to knowing him, she really didn't understand how much latitude an imagination could have.

"We will do a death-defying oriental tumbling act for the benefit of the next passing car."

DeeDee could see a car half a mile down the dusty road, a van. That was promising.

"Now listen to me carefully. Timing is everything, Me Ling. I'm going to kneel down by this sign, and I want you to crawl up my back and perch on my shoulders. I'll pull myself up and prance around by the side of the road while you stick your thumb out. You need to sing something, Me Ling, do you know anything in Chinese by any chance?"

Me Ling's eyes stretched wide; she spoke slowly. How she feared heights. She placed her hand on Dodo's shoulder. "The only song I can remember is 'Always.' Is that good enough?"

"Quick! Up, Me Ling, up! Where is the spirit of Genghis Khan or Chairman Mao?"

Her skinny body crawled up his back, her elbows and knees sticking out in all directions. As he stood up, she felt herself rise up towering, uneasily over the road. She held on to his ears.

The van was now a block away. "Sing now, May Ling, sing my Pekingese songbird!" He began kicking up his legs.

From high in the sky came a thin nervous voice, "I'll be loving you...always. With a love that's true...always. When you're in a jam..."

The van squealed to a stop. Dodo was so excited that he forgot that he was keeping balance for two.

"And need a helping *hand*!"

DeeDee toppled to the ground, almost taking Dodo's left ear with her.

She rubbed her right elbow and he his left ear as they sprawled out on that hot road in the middle of nowhere, and then they ran to catch their ride.

A truck zoomed by interrupting her reverie, and she was back with Leonard sitting outside that station looking up that maddening hill.

The city of Taormina was still towering above them out of reach. The irritatingly lavender flowered bougainvillea, which draped the mountain on which their refuge stood, seemed to tease them. An occasional prickly pear cactus broke through those seductive vines to remind Leonard and Frannie that they weren't going anywhere.

There future was blocked by an unbreachable summit all extravagant and bristly. Frannie stood up and looked up the road with longing. It wound up impossibly steep to finally disappear into that reluctant promise of a city on top.

All the time, the sun was setting, and she knew once again that they would enter a shadowy damp city and wander around in the dark looking for some place to sleep.

She stopped staring upward, yanked her suitcase closer, and sat on it again. She slipped off her shoe and rubbed her heel with sullen intensity.

Leonard kept up his stiff sentry duty. He too had stopped looking up and was now fixing his gaze on the road immediately ahead in a determined attempt to materialize a bus.

Neither talked to each other as the bright sun was moving behind the hill. Frannie could already feel the chill setting in.

One of the cars scrambling up the hill stopped. A weathered-looking man looked out at the stranded pair. His arm with hairs glistening in the last of the daylight was casually hanging out of the opened window. He smiled at them, a big yellow-toothed pirate smile. "Signor and Signora." He bowed slightly.

Frannie looked up at that gleaming smile as if the sun was moving back up in the sky. She gave a little gasp of pleasure; yes, he was a taxi driver.

144

"Scusi, Signora, you and signor…need ride to city?"

Frannie looked at Leonard almost as excited as if she had been riding on his shoulders.

Leonard glanced disapprovingly at the driver. "There's a bus coming soon…" He looked back at the road, his pride intact.

Frannie's face began going limp. "I'm sorry, signor. I guess we'll wait for the bus."

The taxi looked at Frannie still smiling. "Bus, signora?"

"We're sure the bus is coming. At least it is supposed to be… anytime now, isn't it, Leonard?"

Leonard nodded his head without actually joining the conversation.

The driver looked at them quizzically and said something in very rapid Italian. Inside the car, he lifted both his hands up with a bewildered gesture and drove off, leaving a little cloud of exhaust from his rattling car.

The two were absolutely silent.

Finally, Frannie shifted slightly on the suitcase and put her shoe back on with a strange intensity. "Leonard…Leonard."

He nodded his head again but didn't look in Frannie's direction.

"Leonard. We have to do something soon, don't you think? I don't think that bus is going to come. It's getting dark. I hate getting into town again when it's dark."

"Frannie, what do you want me to do? I can't make the bus come." He shot a tight-lipped look at her.

"Maybe the bus isn't going to ever come."

"You're always complaining. I never do anything right."

"I didn't say that. I just meant why don't we take a cab up?"

"The bus is supposed to come! If you'd just be patient for once."

"But what if it doesn't come, and we just sit here all night?"

"Don't you think I'm smart enough to get us up there? A lot of help you are."

"Oh, I didn't mean to say anything against what you're doing. You do everything so well, Leonard. You take such good care of me."

He was giving her the silent treatment now.

"You really do take such good care of me, Leonard, but my feet hurt again, and I would love to take my shoes off and relax."

He glanced over at her for an instant. "I suppose if you're feet are getting sore, we can take a taxi. The bus will come, but for you, Frannie, I'll get a taxi."

"Thank you, darling."

Within minutes, Leonard spotted another rattling taxi and waved it over.

The next morning, Frannie woke first. Leonard seemed so tired; perhaps this trip was taking a toll on him too. Naked she quietly sat up, grabbed a bathrobe that she had laid across a chair, and slipped it on.

The morning sun squeezed through the horizontal cracks of the window shutter like a brilliant ladder to heaven. She walked across the cool marble floor, undid the latch, and opened the shutters a few inches. Her robed form was floodlit in the morning sun, her hair a frizzy halo. She looked out and gasped. She was a bird perched on a tower, perched up in the dizzy sky, below a city, and far, far below a sea. Her robe fell open, revealing herself to the morning. For a second, she forgot about the sleeping man in the room and opened the shutters wide, spreading her arms out as if in flight—a flight into the impossible blue.

She heard the springs of the bed creak. She turned around to her spouse. "Oh, my dear, I'm so sorry I woke you. I'm intoxicated by the sea and the sky. It is so lovely."

Leonard, staring into the brilliant light, could only see Frannie's shadowed silhouette. He jumped up and out of the bed like a guard found sleeping at his post. "So much to do today. There's a Roman theater on the edge of town. It overlooks the scenic bay. From the distance, you can see Mount Etna. There is supposed to be a lovely garden that the English established at the turn of the century. English gardens are particularly fine. We'll grab some coffee and start our day. Aren't you afraid that somebody will see you standing there with your bathrobe open?"

The dark form set against the sunshine began approaching him. "I'm giving the Italians a treat." As she stepped farther into the room he could see that she was smiling, smiling at him. She dropped her robe and kissed him as she slipped into bed.

Unfortunately, Taormina was a rather unsatisfactory place. Leonard said that there were far too many tourists. Tourists, after all, are flighty, flimsy creatures; and Leonard, of course, was made of sterner stuff. He was there for serious reasons. If only he could find a satisfactory place, he could actually get down to the serious business of living in Italy like a real Italian.

As Leonard and Frannie walked through the city that day, he pointed out all the cheap bric-a-brac that was being sold at the storefronts that lined many of the streets. "When the English discovered this place, it was so authentic. Now they have ruined all these old stone buildings, making them into stores and even discos."

She nodded at him in deep sympathy. She noticed though how flowers were growing everywhere, especially where they were not intended to be—pink snapdragons scattered themselves over the hoary ruins of temples, a red flowering plant of some sort poked its way through niches in walls; and the bougainvillea vines flowering in shades of lavender draped itself across walls and hung down in tresses from the stone archways. She saw crimson flowered geraniums growing unbidden below laundry, waving on lines that extended over the narrow streets, flapping, and catching the sun liked tethered birds. "Yes…I suppose so…maybe."

They stepped down a narrow cobbled road and through a high arch.

The city was straddling the side of its mountain. Stony buildings clustered on the steep inclines pile upon pile of houses like stepping-stones always going up. Hard to imagine people living ordinary lives in those aeries up against the sky.

Frannie and Leonard walked through a narrow passageway and stepped out onto a kind of small open plateau, a precious flat space that hung out over the bay. They were in a garden. Hibiscus trees still had a few of their blooms in mid-November.

There were extravagant banana trees with their long broad leaves that seemed to push up with such irresistible force. Frannie could almost see them growing. There were large outdoor cages of exotic birds that she had never seen before. Everywhere were beds of plants, some even flowering this late in the year.

"By the way, Frannie, we have to move out of the pensione tomorrow. When I spoke to the desk clerk, she said that they were closing up for the season."

"They're closing up?"

The scenery suddenly flattened out for her...more travel, more nights getting off the train to find a small room to stay in a town that never seemed quite right.

"What if all these little towns on the coast are closing, where will we stay?"

Perhaps it was the memory of Frannie lowering herself into the bed with him this morning without even being asked; he put a hand out and touched her shoulder in a moment of comfort. Then it was back to business as usual.

"Before we leave, we need to see the Greek theater. It should be right ahead. Then we'll move on. We wouldn't want to stay here anyway, too many tourists."

"Yes, Leonard." She took his hand.

November 17, 1996

We made it back across the bay of Messina on a ferry and took a train up the west side of Italy. Day by day now the weather gets a little chillier. The sky is gray today with big bloated clouds that sometimes drop rain.

The train followed the coast. It looked rocky and barren except for the stone houses and olive orchards scattered at the bases of mountains.

Olive trees looked so silvery, almost metallic as they shook their leaves in the ghostly autumn wind.

And there were tiny towns. To me, they looked kind of sad and vulnerable huddled each on its own little mountain so exposed to the threatening weather. The sea no longer seemed turquoise but was gray and choppy. The very few people who were on the train seemed silent and forlorn.

Finally, the train turned inland a bit; the land was flatter, and there were more farms and sometimes little restaurants and old women carrying bags up and down the roads.

Suddenly we were on the outskirts of a larger town with ramshackle buildings cluttered on crisscrossing roads.

It was evening and starting to rain, so deserted looking...Tropea.

Even Leonard seemed to be wearing out. He slept in some mornings. Sometimes he even napped in the afternoon. I tried to comfort him when he was like that, a lost soul. Strange, I liked him better when he looked lost. He seemed all vulnerable, like a little boy. I called him Lennie, and for a few moments, I felt tenderness toward him.

I think we were the only residents of this cavernous hotel in Tropea. It felt like the end of the world here, just Leonard, myself, and that silent little man in black who showed us our room without looking at us. We, the last three people on earth, resided in this grand hotel by the sea, and the sea was dark and wild. The sound of breaking, grinding waves echoed through the marble halls, screaming, "*Doom!*" I think I was getting a little carried away.

Funny how Italians make so many of their buildings out of stone. I guess not so funny; stones seem to be something that Italians have a lot of.

The marble floors here are quite wonderful even if the ceilings are so low that the grand chandeliers skim the top of my head. Why do I have to be so tall?

Shorter women are so much cuter. I was never cute. Yes, Mom, I know if I stand up straight, boys might like me even though I am so ungainly.

This place felt haunted. After the sullen manager showed us to our room, I opened the shutters to look out at the sea. It was churning out there, and I could hear the rain making desolate rattling sounds on the roof.

There are filmy white curtains on the window, and they blew into the room like ghosts.

Leonard was in bed already, pretending to sleep. For some strange reason, I left the shutters and even the windows open; tonight I didn't want to hide from the windy night.

Years ago, I read how Ulysses had himself tied to the mast of his ship. He had all the other sailors put wax in their ears. Then his ship steered past the islands where beautiful sirens perched on fatal rocks beckoning sailors to their deaths.

That night, I listened to the sounds too. I crawled into bed and held Lennie's head against my breast until we both fell asleep.

I woke up early and looked out the open window. The sun was just coming up. It was a clear morning. The air seemed sweet, the curtains gently fluttering. I got up. I didn't even put my bathrobe on; there was no one outside.

I stepped to the window. (I wonder if I was becoming an exhibitionist.) The sky was like a blushing rose, and the sea was a dark aquamarine, but even more impossible, two islands hung out in the distance like mirages suspended between the sea and sky.

Being there in that strange room seemed just fine for a moment. By the time Leonard woke up, the sky was beginning to cloud over again. The desk clerk said that they are closing this place down for the season in two days.

Today while Len napped, I wondered through the town. The clouds here seemed so low. They crowded out the sun with their big dark bellies full of moisture. I wore a jacket.

Leonard didn't think that there were really any important sites here. There were mostly boarded up summer villas around the hotel. Even the town itself was half-closed down. The little shops that sold souvenirs and gelato were boarded up.

I walked toward town; one fish vendor had a few lonely fish spread out on a table in front of his shop. A little farther down there was a butcher shop with a very flushed heavyset man staring out the door, brooding. Just behind him, almost invisible in the shadows of the store, stood a woman in a dark dress wiping a counter down.

A few people passed by on the sidewalk, carrying plastic bags; they scurried by as if at any moment the sky would split open wrecking destruction on the town.

Finally, I had passed through the more modern part of the town. The old city sat up on an elevation of stone that stuck out into the sea. Below the old walls were a cliff, and then a fine sandy beach that in summer must be filled with people from Germany.

My, but all a person has to do to find out how predatory humans are is to travel in Italy. All these towns though walled and elevated bear witness to countless sieges and desperate last days, the conquering and the conquered over and over again, and safety that's only wishful thinking. I suppose it's easier to bake bread and sell fish and have children if you think you are safe, and if not safe, at least right. This cool wet weather is making me morbid.

I walked up some grand stone stairs and past the remnants of some sort of castle tower and found myself crowded in by old buildings. They hung over me, almost blocking out the gray sky, damp moldering plaster on the surface of everything.

I squeezed through those tight buildings for five minutes and found a little piazza. On one end was a dilapidated cathedral that probably never really was grand. The other side of the piazza hung out over a steep ravine that opened toward the sea, which was now a dark ominous green. Those fat-bellied clouds seem to barely be able to make it over the elevated town. The clouds blanketed the towers of the town in gray damp silence. It was so silent that I could hear the soft gurgling of a fountain.

The world was still. In my belly, I felt a kind of cool emptiness, half loneliness and half wonder.

I sat down.

Then two boys on a motor scooter scuttered through the piazza and set everything in noisy motion. A small dog with wiry matted hair shot across the piazza to poke its head through a metal railing sending a skinny black-and-white cat screeching into some raggedy cannas plants that surrounded the small pool with its sputtering fountain; a fountain that rained down on several silent goldfish, which seemed completely oblivious to the commotion. (I think that is the longest sentence I have ever written.)

A bird cawed a stern warning from the ravine. I felt an alarm, like being woken up at five in the morning when it is dark and cold outside, and I know that I have to get ready for work. I'm having a hard time with Leonard.

Another cat screeched and ran into a large metal trash container not so picturesquely placed by the fountain. A complaining orange cat jumped out of that container and very low slung ran across the piazza. It turned its head back in the direction from which it fled and let out a defiant scream before it continued its embarrassed flight; it's not so easy being married.

I feel so alone and disappointed. I'm turning into my mother.

Now the black-and-white cat from the cannas stepped out, not low slung or in flight but in a kind of silent padding sentry duty, silent as the goldfish. A sluggish gecko waited on the wall at the very edge of the precipice waiting for a fly.

In the past, it seemed like I was always waiting for some special man—kind, down-to-earth, and peaceful as the goldfish in the pond; patient as the gecko on the precipice; and even better, dominant as the sentry cat.

But now part of me was just irritated with all the commotion of my dream come true. Irritated with Leonard. Irritated with myself...how I am with him.

Fortunate Fannie Fortunato finally found her fella only to flounder in the foolishness of her own fantasies...*foie*!

Then a small gray bird with a rusty tail and wings so small that they kind of flicker shot up into the air in front of me and blew my cover. When a young man with pop singer hair and a turquoise shirt rode through the piazza on another scooter, everyone could see the middle-aged woman writing.

That night, while a cold rain splashed against the window and the waves outside smashed against the beach, Leonard spent more time than usual rustling through tour books and maps.

Frannie was writing a postcard to Dodo. "Tomorrow off to Sorrento sounds like the perfect place. Leonard says that it's beautiful. I was in the town of Tropea today, daydreaming. I got caught in a downpour. Sorrento is close to Pompeii. Leonard says that they have found fossilized people in Pompeii twisted and frozen with screams still on their lips. As you can see, I'm having a wonderful time."

Frannie looked up for a second and said to no one in particular. "I don't want to go too far north. Every day it seems to get a little colder."

Leonard was totally absorbed in studying the map and didn't look up. To no one in particular, he said, "Capri is just a boat trip away. We have to see Capri."

She started another postcard. "I suppose so."

"I promise we won't go any farther north than that. I'm sure I can find a place in Sorrento to send faxes to the office. I wonder if I really should have left Lawrence to his own devices."

"Devices?"

She was trying to think of something to write to Jean. It had to be different than what she had written to Dodo but equally entertaining. They might compare postcards, and Frannie's reputation for originality was at stake.

"He's a fast learner, but sometimes his judgment..." She lost her train of thought and put down the card. "What sense is it to keep worrying now? We came here to get away, my dear, didn't we?"

"You're being pretty cavalier about our only source of income."

"Cavalier? I gave up my job to come on this holiday of yours."

"That wasn't a job that you had, Frannie. That was a hobby. And I just haven't found the right place yet."

"Maybe I didn't find the right job yet."

"Right job...you don't know what it is to work. You and your absurd hippy ideas." Enough said, he went back to studying his maps. A few minutes later, he looked up again. "Tomorrow they're closing this place for the season. We'll take the train up to Sorrento. It's supposed to be beautiful."

"I suppose so."

At 9:00 p.m., they both silently took off their clothes and crawled between the clammy sheets. Only the sound of rain splattering against the window and the churning sea filled the room. No opened windows tonight.

Then "Good night, Lennie" came from Frannie's covered form as she hugged her side of the bed.

"Good night, Frannie," muttered the lump on Leonard's side.

Then more rain and that lonely sea sound. The damp chill of the night penetrated that bed.

"Tell me about Sorrento, Lennie. It sounds beautiful."

That lump on Leonard's side of the bed moved. "It sits high above the Bay of Naples, and it's full of important sights. We can take day trips to Naples or Pompeii. We'll be happy there."

Frannie turned toward his form. She patted his shoulder softly. "Sounds lovely, my dear."

CHAPTER 19

LEONARD GOT UP first that morning to check the maps. Once again, he looked resolute; plans bombarded the tight expressionless face of his.

Frannie too was back to a more usual routine, sleeping as long as she could in the face of all the changes of the day. After all, a journey north up the coast to Sorrento faced them today.

They had coffee and bread with butter and jam at a table in the empty dining room. The waiter, who was probably the owner, brought the two cups of coffee out to them and then quite unexpectedly almost warmly said, "Taxi, need taxi?"

Before Leonard could look offended, Frannie jumped in. "*Gratias,* signor."

They lugged their bags down the silent marble corridors and down a small shuddering elevator and paid the bill; and sure enough, there stood a taxi that carried them through the town that in daylight.

The sky was grayish blue, and the air was soft. They pulled their suitcases into the shabby little station on the outskirts of town and walked to the barred window of the ticket seller.

Once again, a conversation went on between the ticket seller and Leonard, perhaps incomprehensible not only to Frannie.

Leonard kept saying, "Sorrento, Sorrento!"

The ticket seller kept saying, "Salerno, Salerno!"

It was Leonard's turn again. "No! Sorrento, Sorrento!"

The arias of the two voices were building to a crescendo.

Occasionally their increasingly excited voices joined into a duet. Finally, the ticket seller simply filled out tickets to Salerno, slapped them on the counter, and pushed them under the grate.

Frannie watched the men stare at each through the bars while the two tickets sat there ready to be taken. Finally, Frannie's hand very gently crept up to the counter. She touched the ticket,\ and then looked into the teller's eyes and with supplication said, "Sorrento?"

The teller relaxed his face and as if talking to a child and said, "*No possibile.*"

Frannie shook her head and repeated, "No possible."

The teller smiled and began explaining something in rapid Italian.

Frannie listened as if she understood. Her hand still rested on the tickets as if she was afraid that one of the men would somehow deprive her of their possibility.

Now she looked up at Leonard with supplication. "Perhaps we can get to Sorrento from Salerno. When we get to Salerno, we can buy the tickets?"

There was a moment of silence.

Leonard let out a huff of air and passed money under the grate. He picked up the tickets without looking at them. Frannie put her hand on Leonard and gave a grateful little squeeze. They lugged their suitcases out to the tracks.

The scene on the platform was much more carefree.

A group of seven or eight young men all neatly dressed in new blue jeans were standing by the outer wall of the station.

One at a time, each would defiantly walk up to the wall and slap it with his hand with all his might. After each sharp slapping sound, all the young men would cheer.

As far as Frannie could tell, the object of the game was to see who could hit the wall hardest without breaking his hand, and clearly, it hurt their hands. After each boy delivered his smacking blow, he would grimace, almost ready to cry until the cheers would buoy him up.

Slap…cheer…slap…cheer…slap…cheer filtered through the soft Italian morning. The slaps seemed to be getting harder.

As each young man positioned himself for the blow, he seemed more and more apprehensive, but the promise of cheers pushed him to a further feat of daring.

About ten feet away sat a group of young women giggling to each other as the young men went through their ordeal. After each slap, the girls would whisper to each other as if they were appraising each blow.

Though neither group seemed to have time to notice anything but the young men's antics, two girls immediately got up as Leonard and Frannie approached them. With very formal gentility, the girls motioned the couple to their bench. Even the boys paused for a minute. As soon as Frannie and Leonard sat down, the boys continued their slapping and the girls their giggling appraisal.

A young man and an older woman walked onto the station platform. Age seems to have carried them across some behavioral watershed; he no longer wore jeans; she no longer giggled. Occasionally in unison (They seemed to do almost everything in unison.), they would glance contemptuously shaking their heads at the slapping, cheering youths. Although on rare stolen moments, the grave young man would sneak a wistful look at the frolicking younger men.

The train pulled up to the station, grinding and clanging to a stop. The slapping game evaporated as the young men and women picked up their schoolbooks and silently filed into the train compartment. The Italian couple followed more gravely; Leonard with Frannie in tow then entered a compartment. The train gave a quick jolt, and all the passengers jerked back a little in their seats; the train began carrying all those passengers to their destination.

Leonard had pulled out one of his maps; Frannie watched the olive trees and stony hills go by. She kept looking out the window as if through sheer concentration, she could materialize a place of rest.

Even when she opened the window to look beyond the glass, the landscape outside seemed as impervious to entrance as a photograph. Somewhere an hour outside of Tropea, the gentle rocking lulled her to sleep.

She woke to the sound of Leonard rustling through his suitcase. Her head was resting on his bunched-up jacket. She smile with her eyes closed as she sat cushioned, cradled by a gentle sense of him; a lemony scent mixed with the smell of damp earth. He must have gently placed it under her head after she had fallen asleep.

She opened her eyes to the window and the telltale signs of a city. Little farms were giving way to gas stations and dingy factories and occasional ugly newer apartment buildings; they were all mixed together in a chaotic and grimy maze that seemed to surround so many cities in southern Italy.

This time, though that area of maze seemed more extensive, the bus winding and halting and winding again through endless twisting streets filled with people complaining and laughing and buying sausage or cheese or fruit from tiny stores that opened out right to the streets.

Occasionally there were tiny patches of orchard or garden that had somehow withstood the expanding grimy sprawl, tattered remnants of a former life.

Leonard solicitously touched her shoulder. "We're approaching Salerno, Frannie. The guidebook doesn't have much good to say about it. We'll take the train to Sorrento from here. Sorrento sounds perfect. You'll see."

From the warm nest of his jacket, Frannie smiled and then sat up. "You are so gallant, my dear. Sometimes I don't think I deserve you."

He smiled reassuringly at her as the train wound its way through two towering apartment buildings with wash hanging from almost every floor. There was the sea again, glinting in the hazy late afternoon sun. Even this far north, the water at the edges of the bay was turquoise; she wanted to stay in place colored turquoise. Up ahead pushing its way up and through the urban debris rose a city of some size, a city by a turquoise bay.

She rubbed her eyes for a minute, certainly sleep must be playing tricks on her; just beyond the city towered a strange almost vertical ridge of worn limestone cliffs etched in fantastic shapes.

As the train got closer, she saw that the city was nestled up against that strange barrier that seemed to block farther progress north. As she studied it, she saw that it was a whole massive peninsula jagged and elevated that rose up behind Salerno. The city seemed to hover at the base, at the mercy of that wild mass that hung above it, ponderous and impenetrable.

It was midafternoon, and the sun was edging toward that huge mass of rock that jutted out into the sea. As the train drew nearer, it was joined by more and more tracks. There was an odd sense of finality as if there was no going beyond this point, and by default, that barrier provided, if not a destination, at least an end.

The train was solemnly slowing now; passengers began grabbing paper parcels tied up with string from the compartments above them. In slow motion, a sign with "Salerno" written on it sailed across the window.

The train stopped, gave one quick forward jolt, and the doors opened. The train trip was over.

With bags and parcels and suitcases, people filed out the door, each driven by some compelling purpose, all except for Leonard and Frannie. Though Leonard had managed to push Frannie and himself out in the vanguard, once out the platform, even Leonard seemed at a loss, this was Salerno, the place that wasn't supposed to be.

They stood silently by their pile of luggage while people filed around them urgently. As the platform finally cleared, some sense of purpose seemed to have been rekindled in Leonard; he once again charged into the lead, ushering Frannie across the platform and down an underground passage in which those rivers of people had disappeared.

She marveled at her husband's sense of direction. They walked upstairs now and found themselves in a cavernous marble station.

The sound of clustered people rapidly talking filled that space with echoes. Unerringly Leonard approached a ticket booth. Frannie was pulling her suitcase two steps behind him.

A middle-aged man with a crisp white shirt and black suspenders sat behind the bars of the booth. His even blacker hair was precisely slicked down. Glasses with frames, even blacker than his hair, were perched low enough on his nose so that he could look over them with grave official disapproval.

He was rapidly stamping tickets and sending passengers on their way. Leonard and Frannie positioned themselves at the end of the fast-moving line. Leonard had charge of the maps and guidebooks, and she was responsible for pushing their pile of luggage behind him as the line moved.

It was the awaited moment now. Leonard approached the bars of the window, and the black-haired ticket seller was already beginning to look ominously over his glasses. Leonard began speaking in Italian. Half way through Leonard's sentence, the man behind bars simply shook his head and, with a flick of his hand, said, "No!" and started talking to the next man in line.

Leonard simply stood there without budging like an immovable object obstructing any further business at the window. Rather magisterially he placed his hand on the ticket counter and said, "Sorrento! Sorrento!"

Without taking his eyes off the next customer, the ticket teller simply shot out the words "Autobus! Autobus!" and continued with the transaction occurring over Leonard's body, which seemed frozen in place.

Frannie's tentative hand reached out to Leonard's shoulder. He looked so much like some boy who couldn't believe that he had just lost a very important game.

"I think maybe he means we have to take the bus from here to get to Sorrento. I saw all those mountains up ahead, and maybe the train can't go through them?"

Leonard turned from the scene of his humiliation toward Frannie. "The guidebook says that we can take the train to Sorrento. *That* man just won't listen to me. There's supposed to be a train to Sorrento!"

She tried to look very sympathetic and maybe a little outraged at his fate. "Yes, I know. I saw it too. Maybe that guidebook is wrong."

Leonard face softened slightly, relieved that someone had the sense to know that the guidebook, not he, was wrong. He had been judged innocent.

"When I get back to the States, I am going to write to that publisher and let him know what trouble he has caused us."

Though Frannie kept nodding urgently, he continued to stand in front of the ticket booth; his remaining sense of purpose directed at the future punishment of the offending author.

She put her hand over his. "Let's go sit down for a second, Leonard, and look at that stupid old guidebook. Maybe we can figure out what we want to do." Then she smiled. "We are certainly having our adventure."

He looked at her with something almost like admiration.

They found an empty bench in that crowded station that two young lovers who had been kissing each other had just vacated.

While people were rushing around, Leonard grabbed the offending guidebook. He held it tentatively as if it no longer merited complete trust. He studied it, his face gradually taking on his more usual tight-lipped expression. "The book says that we can also take a bus at a station a block or two away. The bus proceeds up and through that rugged peninsula and through some small picturesque towns until it reaches our destination, Sorrento. Someone really should have checked this book more carefully. We'll pass through that series of small towns. One of them is called Amalfi. The book says that someone wrote a play about a duchess who was imprisoned and murdered there. Sounds like a very grim story. A little farther is a town called Positano. The guidebook says that John Steinbeck lived there for a while. Those towns are much too small to stay in, but it will make an interesting tour." He set the guidebook down on his suitcase.

Frannie, heartened by her foray into resourcefulness, took up the book and opened it. "Amalfi, a small seaside resort town perched on limestone cliffs with a turquoise bay beneath. This historic town was the home of the duchess of Amalfi, who was murdered with her children by her vengeful brothers for secretly marrying a commoner. The tower where they were murdered still overlooks the town today."

"Leonard, let's spend a night in Amalfi, maybe even a couple of days. It sounds so romantic. Maybe we'll like it enough to stay there."

"Don't be so impulsive, Frannie. It's just a tiny town, probably closing up for the winter like all the rest."

"Oh please, Leonard, please. It sounds so lovely, and maybe it'll be big enough. Oh, how I would just love to stop for a while…how horrible to murder a mother and her children!"

He paused a moment, took the guidebook back, and said, "I'll stop there just for you."

"I want to walk up to the tower. You're a dear."

They set off, two middle-aged travel-worn people, pulling their big suitcases down the sidewalks and across the roads of Salerno while little cars beeping their horns shot around them.

Frannie, in particular, had to be careful as she wheeled her wobbly suitcase. At any moment, it seemed ready to pitch over and topple into the path of the cars or collide with those fast-paced people with lovely shoes who pressed in around her.

At one particularly towering curb which Frannie was trying to surmount, just as she and the suitcase were losing their balance, an old man in a dusty-looking black suit, smoking a cigarette, suddenly hoisted up the faltering back of the suitcase. There he was behind her, smelling of cigarettes and some earthier smell, smiling at her in deep satisfaction over their joint triumph. They stood, looking at each other—an island of familiarity in that rushing river of city commotion.

Instead of introducing himself to the distressed damsel, he simply took a slow drag from the cigarette hanging from the side of his mouth, released a small cloud of smoke, and said, "To autobus?" She smiled apologetically. "My husband and I are going to Amalfi."

He took another drag of his cigarette and blew out a long smoky sigh. "Amalfi, Bella Amalfi, Bella!" He flicked ashes off his cigarette, staring off into the distance as if he was actually experiencing the delights of that fair town.

Frannie leaned on the suitcase toward him. Her tone became confidential. "Yes, I mean *si*. I have never been very good at languages, not that I don't like people, but you know, I barely can understand what people say in my own language. Italian really does sound beautiful, except I wish people wouldn't speak so fast."

He looked at her with benign incomprehension. Then he motioned over his shoulder and once again said, "To autobus?"

Frannie was still in a confidential mode but looked just a tad embarrassed. "I suppose that you don't understand a thing I'm saying. I know it must seem silly that I suddenly need to talk to someone when I have a perfectly good husband. Oh, I'm sorry, yes, I mean si, autobus…si, autobus."

He looked so thrilled to be finally comprehended that he dropped his cigarette and began pantomiming taking money out of his pocket and buying something. "*Si, signora, bigletta a stazione.*"

So close yet so far, she understood *si*. She understood *signora*, but the rest of what he was saying…why, that was a different story.

Bigletta sounded like it might have something to do with buying letters perhaps.

Like some explorer sailing out into unknown seas, she set out from the port of the few Italian words that she could understand: *signor*. She paused apprehensively finding herself in deep water. Then she was buoyed up by hope. "Buy letter? Do I want to mail a letter? How kind of you, but I don't think so. I usually send postcards."

He now waved his right hand back and forth with some urgency and said, "No, no, no."

Meanwhile Leonard, who had been moving steadily and intrepidly forward, turned around to find his wife well behind him in the throng of moving people, engaged in a spirited conversation with a stranger. Suitcase and all he struggled back upstream just in time to hear the old Italian say once again but more urgently, "*Bigletta por autobus…stazione!*"

Leonard intervened, "Frannie, *bigletta* means ticket. I think he means we buy the ticket for the bus at the station."

The old man took out another cigarette and said, "*Si, si, bigletta por autobus a stazione*" and began waving a little wildly at a building down the block.

"Oh, isn't that wonderful, Leonard, all the time he was trying to tell us where to go." With her absolutely most gracious smile, she reached her hand toward that stranger like a queen bestowing knighthood. "*Gracia*, signor, very *gracias*."

He smiled back at her pleased as a papa and once again uttered, "Bella, Bella Amalfi!" and disappeared into the moving crowd.

"What a wonderful old man, Leonard. I think Amalfi will be a good idea."

"You wait right here, don't move. Do you hear me? Don't move. I'll go and see if that's the station. You never know if you can trust a person." He left his bags with her, and she seemed quite content sitting on her island of luggage with chaos rushing around her.

And Frannie loved buses almost as much as hitchhiking—the intimate dimness inside, the public brightness out, but most of all, the smell, the way the aroma of gasoline, and the scent of old perfume mixes with just a hint of human urgency. By the time the two stepped up and on the bus, the shadowy seats were almost filled with rustling talking people. How wonderful!

Almost as soon as they got seated, a slim bus driver in a very elaborate uniform leaped onto the bus armed with a notepad and a swashbuckling smile. Voices called out to him, "Andrea! Andrea!" He casually saluted the crew of his ship and in rapid Italian fired what seemed like enthusiastic questions to various shadowy people. Still talking, he turned and sat down on his pilot's seat and flicked the engine on.

The bus rumbled, shuttered, and set out into the sunset or at least into the late afternoon.

Still throwing questions to the passengers behind him, he cavalierly piloted that large bus through the narrow streets filled with traffic. They were off not only to the sunset but to those wild looking limestone cliffs looming above them.

Frannie, whose own sense of personal geographic placement was tentative, to say the least, marveled at the bus drivers surety of space as if he had some sixth sense by which he could locate himself and actually move uninjured through the bustling chaos that filled the roads of Salerno.

At first, the bus darted around and immersed in the crowded narrow streets, but Frannie noticed how it kept looping back and forth, and with each loop up another street, the bus was gradually ascending, climbing up layers of the city. She looked out the window; the town and the bay were beneath them now and up ahead were impossibly steep cliffs. She tried to peer ahead to find the buses pathway, but all she could see was the narrow road disappearing into that cliff face that pushed out into the sea.

She closed her eyes for second; the bus was about to take off, pointing its nose up toward the limestone cliffs. Instinctively she reached out toward Leonard's knee, and then in midair, her hand stopped and moved on back to her own lap.

This trip was her idea. Her eyes opened wide, and she looked straight out the window. The bus was zigzagging now, scaling up into the towering peninsula. The sea was at a dizzy distance below.

When she looked out the window on her side of the bus, she saw endless blue. When she looked out the window on the other side of the bus, she saw the limestone cliff pressing in almost shoving the bus off its perch. She felt like some young bird being pushed out of a nest.

Then her daring deserted here. She moved back toward the center of the bus, toward Leonard, and sat very still. She just knew that any sudden movement on her part would topple the bus sending it down crashing into the sea, down, down into the sea. She placed her hand on his knee and gripped tightly.

After several frozen minutes, curious person that she was, she began peeking out of the cliff through the side window and noticed how tiny plants, some even with flowers, were growing out of even the steepest incline, out of any nook and cranny that a seed could settle into.

Suddenly the bus lurched to the right as if it was going to actually tunnel into the rocky barrier. She looked ahead and noticed that the road was following a little jagged inlet into the cliff, a little loop into the land.

From a distance, the peninsula looked like a monolithic barrier, but now she could see that that barrier was actually made of coves and mountains pushing out toward the sea. Down below, she forced herself to look, was a bit of sandy beach and a littler turquoise bay.

All up and down that inlet were terraces, lemon trees hanging in gardens going up into the sky; some even brushed the sides of the bus. When she looked closely, she saw narrow walkways snaking steeply up the terraces. Tiny houses perched, scattered up and down the green sides of that steep little valley.

Every inch of land was covered in narrow garden plots and orchards. The bus lurched again. It had gone as far as it could go inland and now was traveling along the other side of the bay heading straight out into the sea again.

The bus made a sudden stop on the cliff side. An old woman in a warm-looking black dress stood up and grabbed a box from overhead. Though she pulled it down rapidly, all the while talking to someone across the aisle, her movements seemed precise almost graceful, a rapid dance in which she avoided hitting anyone with her large parcel.

"Ciao, Maria. Ciao, Therese."

The shadowy figures she left behind called out, "Ciao, Angela." And then with unquestionable dignity, she walked to the front of the bus, said something softly to the bus driver, and stepped down the stairs to the road, which precariously perched against the cliff.

As the bus took off again, Frannie noticed the old woman quickly walked up one of those precipitous pathways that climbed up the green cliff.

The bus was once again pitching rapidly toward the sky and sea as if it was taking a running leap.

Frannie's stomach lurched, and her grip tightened on Leonard's knee. Just as she was sure that this time the bus would actually dive off, sailing and then crashing into the sea, the bus took a sharp turn and again was heading into another tiny valley terraced with orchards. This time, the valley was a little wider; there was actually a town below that seemed to spill out of the narrow valley onto the beach of another turquoise bay. She was sure, just sure that her trip was over, and this was her destination, Amalfi.

Although truth be told, she didn't notice the tower—the tower of the duchess. How would she actually know which town was Amalfi?

Though Leonard was allowing her to clutch his knee, he seemed curiously quiet as he sat on the seat next to her.

A little frantically she bent across the aisle, practically falling off her seat until she caught the attention of a woman about her own age, dressed in a tailored suite of green, a spring green. "Amalfi, Amalfi?"

Frannie pointed down toward the town to which the bus was winding.

At first, it looked like the woman in green was only going to stretch out her hand long enough to steady wobbling Frannie without even stopping her conversation with an older woman sitting next to her. But after the woman in green had successfully steadied Frannie, the woman looked at her with the solicitude. She spoke very clearly and slowly, "No Amalfi…Maiore. No Amalfi."

Perhaps it was that hand touching her shoulder at the exact right moment to prevent a mishap. Frannie bestowed her undivided trust onto the stranger.

The stranger's eyes rested on the American and gave a quick reassuring nod. Frannie nodded back desperately.

The stranger nodded back again, this time with even more soothing reassurance, and then with a sweeping gesture, he motioned Frannie to remain seated.

Frannie was still nodding.

The stranger very definitely pointed out the window and shook her head with an exaggerated motion. "No Amalfi. No Amalfi." She paused and looked Frannie straight in the eye.

Frannie's whole face began to relax as if the stranger's reassurance was beginning to hit the mark.

Then something almost miraculous happened.

It was clear from the bright look on Frannie's face that some information was filtering through her frenzied brain, and some idea was being born. She smiled at the stranger with excited but tentative comprehension. This time, Frannie pointed out the window, shaking her head and said, "No Amalfi, no Amalfi."

The stranger gave a very composed and satisfied nod to Frannie and mentioned something to the older woman next to her. The older woman nodded to Frannie. The younger woman in spring green then very clearly and slowly pointed toward the general direction that the bus was following and said, "Amalfi." Then with that pointing hand, she waved it attempting to indicate distance.

Frannie imitated the motion with her hand while pointing ahead and said, "Amalfi." Comprehension dawned on her face. "Amalfi is farther ahead. Amalfi…ahead. Amalfi…ahead."

The woman looked a little confused. "Amalfi…a head?"

"Yes, Amalfi…ahead."

The young woman pointed her finger to her head and said, "A head?"

As the bus started rapidly winding up another cliff toward the sky, Frannie began laughing as if she had suddenly discovered some cosmic irony. She pointed to her head and said, "A…head," distinctly pausing between those two words. Then she paused even longer before saying, "Ahead," squishing those syllables together and making that far off waving gesture that the stranger had made. "My head." Once again, she pointed to her head, and then she said, "Amalfi ahead," and waved off into the distance.

The young woman looked quizzically at Frannie's moving hand, and then she too started laughing. She pointed to her head and said quite formally, "A…head," with great satisfaction. She pointed up the road and said, "Amalfi…ahead."

In very slow and loud English, as if the louder she spoke the clearer the meaning would be, Frannie said, "My name Frannie." She pounded on her chest for emphasis.

The younger woman still laughing looked at her and very solemnly said, "My name Rina."

"How wonderful! Such a pretty name, Rina." Frannie motioned over to Leonard. "Look, Leonard, I'm speaking Italian." She turned back to her new friend and said, "Rina." Then she pointed to Leonard and said, "Leonard." In a very confidential tone, she said to Leonard, "Rina was just telling me that the last town wasn't Amalfi, but that it is farther ahead. Then she turned to Rina and said, "Merci."

Frannie heard a voice coming from Leonard's direction saying, "Oh, Frannie, that's French."

Her jubilation shattered in embarrassment. "Oh, I'm sorry. I thought I was doing so well."

Rina tilted her head to the side to catch Frannie's downcast eyes. Rina smiled and said, "Merci. Gratias. Thank…you. We teach each other. I go to Amalfi."

Frannie's whole face opened up into a smile. "Gratias, Rina."

Rina said, "Thank…you, Frannie," and once again began conversing with the older woman next to her.

Even though Frannie didn't have the slightest idea what the two women were talking about, she settled back into the reassurance of their company. For the next thirty minutes, the bus kept winding in and out between the mountains and the sky.

Occasionally Frannie would sneak down to see the sea far below rippling into forever; the sky was turning from a pale, liquid blue to a darker aquamarine. Now the sun was edging, dipping down behind the cliffs, leaving shadows.

The bus began looping down to another small bay. A tiny town rested on the bit of beach at the bottom. Already it was completely in shadow.

Frannie, sitting on the edge of the seat, fixed her eyes on Rina. Pausing in her conversation with the older woman, Rina turned to Frannie. She put her arm out to signal wait. "Not Amalfi. Amalfi ahead."

Frannie slid back into her chair, saying, "Gratias." She turned to Leonard and very knowingly said, "This isn't Amalfi yet either. That's what Rina said."

Leonard looked at her a little suspiciously over his glasses. He was busy reading a report that he was planning to send to Thomas.

The bus descended, finally reaching that little town on the beach. The bus squeezed through white stucco houses that were piled one on top of the other, pressing against the narrow road.

A mother with two children stepped out of the bus, the three carried parcels that were in proportion to their sizes: the mother with a gigantic bag of groceries, her oldest daughter, almost a teenager with a medium-sized bag with handles, and finally, the young boy and a small net bag full of lemons.

Then once again, the bus started up the road climbing up and edging its way around a promontory that seemed to stick out far into the sea.

Frannie noticed on the very top of this mountain was a single tower pointing straight up into the darkening sky. The last rays of the sun lit the tower.

Rina turned to Frannie. "Scusi, Frannie, Amalfi…tower of Amalfi…you know story?"

Again, Frannie spoke in an ever so slow and loud voice, "Yes, I...know...Leonard...told me...duchess killed." She pantomimed an expression of first horror and then sadness.

Rina looked back with sadness as if that tragic event had happened yesterday not seven hundred years ago. They shared an odd moment of sympathy. Finally, Rina said, "You stay long...Amalfi?"

Leonard folded his papers precisely and took charge of the conversation. "We are only going to spend a night, just long enough to see the sights. We're moving on to Sorrento. It's so much bigger. Frannie and I have to be in a bigger city. I have business contacts to maintain."

Rina nodded very deferentially and then, with the slightest edge of insistence in her voice, said, "Amalfi bella."

Frannie repeated, "Bella Amalfi."

Rina flashed a smile at Frannie as if she was a very good student. "*Bella*...you say in English...*beautiful?*"

Frannie turned away from her husband. "Yes, beautiful. It is so beautiful here."

The three became silent as the bus began veering around the promontory.

The tower now was out of sight looming above them. There stretching down below was a slightly larger bay. The water was shadowy with streaks of white foam near the beach. Though the town spilling out of that limestone cleft was in deep shadow, the white stucco houses piled up one on top of the other glowed with the memory of day.

The bus gathered momentum as it rushed down to the heart of Amalfi, rapidly shimmying passed stores and houses and finally driving right down to the beach where there was actually a flat empty space covered in asphalt. The bus stopped, and the voices throughout the bus grew louder as shadowy figures searched and found their parcels and bags.

With a quiet pride, Rina motioned out the window to the town beyond. "Amalfi!"

Leonard was straining his eyes in the evening gloom, studying the guidebook intensely.

Rina handed a card to Frannie, not secretly exactly but in that odd private physical way by which Italians seem to communicate with each other; no clumsy words necessary. Quite definitely she nodded to Frannie. Rina turned back to the older woman and then to Frannie and Leonard. "This...my mother...we live...in Amalfi." Then with elegant composure, both women stepped up from their seats and disappeared out the door.

Frannie slipped the card into the notebook that had been sitting on her lap and stared at their vanishing forms.

Leonard broke the spell. "The guidebook says that Hotel Amalfi is inexpensive and quite adequate. There is a central piazza that is supposed to be picturesque and a duomo of some interest."

"Oh yes. I'm sure."

"We'll only be here for one night, so we'll need to be organized for tomorrow."

Frannie was now staring out the window, up across the bay, to that tower at the summit of the cliff, like some dark finger pointing into the evening sky. "Let's go up to the tower Leonard, let's?"

"We'll see if we have time. According to the guidebook, it's in ruins." Leonard seemed to be perking up with the prospect of organizing the next day.

Despite Frannie's dawdling, he managed to get them out of the bus, not exactly first but at least not last.

He led the march to Hotel Amalfi, Frannie following him with her wobbling suitcase. They walked across the parking lot.

The town of Amalfi hung before them, like an impenetrable mass of white that seemed to stop the gap between two mountains. In the gathering, gloom lights were switching on in the city hanging over them.

For a moment, Frannie thought those lights seemed to climb right up into the sky. Resolutely Leonard identified a tunnel that burrowed into that white pile of a city. The two stepped into the shadowy tunnel. Disembodied voices and footsteps of fellow travelers rose out of the darkness.

Leonard rushed through; Frannie lagged, looking backward clumsily, pulling her wildly wobbling suitcase over the rough cobblestones. She was too busy with her suitcase to notice the bright lights at the end of the tunnel.

Head down and looking backward, she stepped out of the tunnel and stopped. She looked up, squinting at the brightness. Suddenly a dazzling childlike smile flashed across her face. She stood in the midst of a brilliantly lit piazza. Storefronts ablaze with light; people sitting around small tables, smiling, and nodding to each other; and the brilliant white stucco of the city rose up around her in an embrace.

The burnt roasted smell of coffee tickled her nose while music spilled out of the open doors of cafes; she spun around, clicking imaginary castanets.

The lovely children all around laughed in wonder at the sight of her. Wrapping herself in the very heart of this hidden city, she looked up, and above the brightness hung the dark shapes of the towering cliffs, and at the peak of one of those dark shapes was the tower pointing its finger into the starry night.

CHAPTER 20

November 19, 1996

Amalfi is like a book that opens. I don't know why I wrote that exactly. I suppose because when I first saw it, it looked like the beautiful cover of some romance novel or at the very least the cover of some tourist guide to Italy: the sea lapping over the gravelly cove and those strange white houses all piled up closing off the space between those wonderful cliffs—cliffs tortured and steep yet hung with what looks like garlands.

They're really groves of lemons. Everything was all so perfect. I hardly wanted to peek inside the town. I could've stay outside the city forever at one of the tourist booths and buy lots of postcards and then leave. I would send them to all my friends and write, "You couldn't imagine how beautiful the city is."

Dreams had always been safer than the messy thing that some people call reality. I called it disappointment. But when that nice Italian woman talked to me on the bus, so far so good.

Just when I was getting my bearings, I spied a very strange fountain at the side of the piazza. Water was shooting out of the nipples of this statue of a naked woman.

Now that wouldn't be so out of the ordinary, I suppose, but towering over her was the statue of a man, not Jesus, because the cross was shaped like an *X*. His limbs were nailed to the cross, but he seemed to be watching the water spouting woman with enjoyment or at least serenity.

Occasionally a man would walk up to those bare spurting nipples and very decorously even religiously take a drink. As if that wasn't quite enough, at the base of the nymph stood several tipsy-looking ducks that appeared to be laughing. If this is reality, there is not much room for disappointment.

Leonard stepped next to me, clearing his throat, motioning with his head toward Hotel Amalfi. I motioned with my head toward the fountain. I told him this was where I want to stay. He looked at me too bewildered to be shocked. He seemed bewildered much of the time now.

I patted him reassuringly on his shoulder, and we lugged our suitcases to our hotel. Leonard kept talking about Sorrento. We'll see about that.

THE NEXT MORNING, Leonard did not have to wake up Frannie. She had things to do, not exactly secret things but just private; she was already writing by the time Leonard got up.

After one cup of coffee and bread with butter and jam, Leonard had a full agenda: a nautical museum, some sort of old paper mill, and of course, the duomo.

Frannie mentioned something about a headache. "Darling, you just go ahead and tell me how everything is. I'm a little under the

weather. I'll just read for a while, and if I get bored, I'll take a little stroll."

Leonard looked bewildered and then was able to muster some
forced resourcefulness. "What's the matter? Aren't you feeling well?
Was the bed too uncomfortable? Would you like me to try another
hotel? I'll stay to take care of you. Have you taken any aspirin?"

"You're such a dear. Why, the hotel is perfect. I just need a little
respite. You go on ahead. I'll be eager to hear about everything. That's
so kind of you, my dear, to want to attend to me, but you just run
along now."

He stepped away with some hesitation. Of late he seemed to
have been developing an absolute penchant for hesitancy. In fact,
the very single-minded Leonard was beginning to pause periodically as if some internal debate was going on, particularly when
Frannie wasn't following his program. He paused, then departed with
some misgivings.

In the silence that he left behind, Frannie began writing again.
As soon as a respectable amount of time went by, she turned the page
to stare at that card that Rina gave her.

> Gorga Travel Agency
> 31 Via Amalfi

Underneath in very hurried writing was a note in pencil.

> Come me to see while you here.

> Rina

Yes, Frannie had an adventure for today too. She closed the
book and slipped the card into a pocket of her blouse. Why, that
little old headache was gone; she was feeling so much better. She
slipped out of the narrow room, down a narrow hallway, passed a
desk behind, which sat a young woman with masses of curly black
hair pulled back from here face.

"*Buon giorno.*"

Frannie smiled and nodded her head slightly but familiarly and said, "Boun giorno," and stepped out into the piazza.

The radiance of the sun on the white buildings sucked the air out of her lungs and overwhelmed her as if she was in a tight embrace.

Finally, she took a deep gasp and closed her eyes—the smells of coffee from a cafe next door and pizza that was being baked somewhere nearby and a sweeter smell too. Yes, there was most certainly a pastry shop here too and then the faint smell of cigarette smoke and the smell of fish from the fish stall and finally the cool salty smell of the Mediterranean.

Voices were calling out, and footsteps beat in rapid syncopation all around her.

Just then the bell of the duomo started ringing, collapsing everything into that resounding peal. Then all up and down the cliffs, other bells were answering, marking the distance of her imagination. She opened her eyes and looked out.

In the midst of that pealing commotion, she looked up to a blue sky so soft and tender that it could break her heart. The light, the light—how could she describe the liquid blue that filled her eyes and brushed her cheeks and filled her with that exact moment.

Yes, this was the place. Columbus may have been audaciously courageous, setting out for America; Marco Polo may have been wildly daring heading toward China, but both their adventures paled in comparison to Frannie's journey to 31 Via 1 d'Amalfi.

This late in the season, there were few other tourists in town, and Frannie did understand that she was a tourist. Perhaps in her life, she had always been a tourist.

A dog, a rather mangy, knowing creature fled up one of the stairways that honeycombed the walls around the piazza. A man sitting next to trays of strange-looking shellfish glanced at Frannie, not with hostility but with the expression of a person who had spent too many months crowded in by tourists.

Another more hopeful man stood amidst his stalls of souvenirs. He smiled and beckoned her to examine his goods. She smiled back but kept walking.

There it was "Via Amalfi" carefully painted on the side of a building; a narrow street ran right underneath the sign. The street emptied out of the piazza into the pile of houses that stretched back into the city squeezing through the white buildings. The towering cliffs on both sides were narrowing and pushing the houses even closer together. The farther she traveled into the town, the more life seemed exquisitely ordinary.

There was a grocery store with goods piled high in its windows.

An old woman in a black dress was standing by the cash register absentmindedly punching out totals, taking money, and bagging groceries. A man who looked suspiciously like her son was pushing huge chunks of sausage through a machine, constructing sandwiches, wrapping them in white paper, and handing them to the people around him who watched and waited.

Older women seemed to fill the streets, dark dressed and businesslike, carrying bags, stopping at the food shops up and down the street, examining the fish or the chicken or the broccoli or the cheese with careful discretion, and firing off complaints or praise before finally making purchases.

The street opened up a little, and there was a small fountain, simply a plaster half shell in the wall out of which a metal tube stuck out dribbling water into a cool basin.

Next to it was a butcher shop that opened into the street.

Frannie listened to the dribbling sound of water and peered into the shadows of the shop, different sized sausages hung over trays filled with large chunks of red meat; the smell salty with just a little underlying odor of sweet decay.

A beefy man with a concentrated look was carefully cutting paper-thin slices from one of the large chunks of meat.

An older woman with a paper bag was watching intently. The older woman complained, "*Basta!*"

Frannie leaned against the plaster wall, powdery and cool. Up above was a strip of tender blue. She walked on, and once again, the street narrowed closing out the sky.

Suddenly she heard a beep behind her. One of those little Italian cars that seemed to scurry around with the fury of an insect hovered directly behind her. The other people in the shadowy alley seemed barely to notice the sound, except that imperceptibly but rapidly they seemed to move to the sides.

While Frannie was thinking it was impossible for that car to squeeze through, she delayed too long, and the car beeped again this time at her. She stared at it with the panic of a prey cornered. The other passage walkers seemed to try not to notice her behavior, except for one old woman who very strictly motioned her over to the side.

The car passed rapidly but delicately through the gap of the alley, and once again, the pedestrians filled the shadowy walkway. Frannie tried to thank the woman, but she had already ducked into a shop with huge golden loaves of bread piled in the window.

Frannie looked backward in the general direction of the bustling piazza. Somewhere back there was Leonard confidently finding his way around the city. She could almost hear a voice from somewhere saying, "But you know Frannie. She has to get lost and almost be run over." In the shadowy ally, her eyes began getting that wild look as if at any moment the whole world might start spinning, and she would fall, fall forever or at least until she was properly humiliated, her frizzy gray-red hair sticking out from her dumbfounded face. "You know Frannie." Those shadowy people who were shuffling passed her must see how preposterous she was.

She suddenly missed that solid form of Leonard marking the trail for her. Her steps were slowing down now. At any moment, her progress would be halted, and she would be carried back to her husband.

Just before inertia completely set in, she saw a sign ahead that said, "Gorga Financial Tours." An arrow pointed up dark stairs that disappeared in the shadowy maze of the city. She heard another beep behind, and she scuttled up the passageway.

Even in the gloom, the white wash on the tunnel walls had an eerie glow. It was such an inevitable tunnel. She didn't even really need foresight to choose her way; once she stepped into it, there was nowhere else to go but up. How simple it all seemed, taking one step and then another into the unknown alone.

A light shone up ahead. She walked toward it and found herself standing on a landing that opened into an office with a large window that hung out over the sunlight street.

There was Rina sitting at a desk with travel posters all around her, talking rapidly into the phone with that kind of ambiguous Italian ferocity that can be either love or hate.

Rina glanced up at her guest between rapid fire sentences and said, "Ciao, Frannie," smiling familiarly as if Frannie had been expected. Then Rina returned to her emphatic conversation, motioning Frannie toward a chair.

Rina hung the phone up and said, "Scusi." She took her glasses off. Her eyes seemed to soften. Her voice lowered in pitch and volume. Her face then tightened a little as she tried to find English words. "My...American friend...you come visit me...excuse my English...you enjoy Amalfi?"

"Oh, Amalfi...I enjoy Amalfi...a beautiful place," Frannie said the word *beautiful* with sparkling emphasis as if she was paying Rina a very personal compliment.

Rina smiled back; compliment accepted. "Thank you. Amalfi... is beautiful."

Frannie echoed, "Amalfi is beautiful," and then smiled like an idiot child.

They both kept smiling and nodding at each other until Rina put her glasses on again. Her tone changed to a more businesslike tone perhaps even calculating. "Frannie...excuse me...do you intend to, how do you say, keep being in Amalfi?"

"Hmm, how would I say it?" Frannie's brows furrowed, her eyes squinted as if she was figuring a complex problem. Suddenly she smiled, relieved. "I would say, 'Are you going to stay in Amalfi a while?'"

Rina nodded very definitely, "You stay in Amalfi for a while."

Frannie looked like a child invited to a birthday party. "Yes, I stay in Amalfi for a while."

Nodding smiles ricocheted between the two women. Rina took charge. "You stay in apartment in Amalfi? You...need apartment... in Amalfi?"

In the excitement of finding herself in a conversation with someone other than Leonard, Frannie forgot to talk in halting English. "Oh yes, I want to. I really don't know about Leonard yet, you know, how men are so fussy." Then she suddenly remembered that she was speaking to a person from another country, and once again, she began talking very slowly with many illogical pauses, "Could you find…us an apartment…here in Amalfi…Amalfi…beautiful."

"Amalfi beautiful…yes…you come tomorrow. I show you apartment…beautiful apartment…bella…you like sea?"

"Oh yes, I love the sea."

"Bella mare!"

"Bella mare!"

CHAPTER 21

THE TOPS OF the jagged cliffs disappeared into dark roiling clouds; dark green waves in the bay thrashed restless against shore. Three figures climbed up a pathway, snaking into the cliffs: two women in the lead and a man following.

Frannie paused, glancing back at Leonard, trudging along behind. Rina stopped on the pathway midway up the cliff. Standing on edge of the precipice, she waved her arm grandly across the bay, "All yours!" As if on cue, bells all over the town below began ringing and mixing with the sound of the restless waves. Frannie looked up, following Rina's waving hand. Rina's hand gave a little flick as if shaking something off it, and Frannie's gaze flew off like a bird across the distant bay and finally settled on the town below.

Leonard, winded, head down caught up with them. "How much farther?"

A veil of exaggerated concern slipped over Frannie's face. Rina's eyes sparkled at Leonard. "Bella Amalfi."

His eyes shot from Frannie to Rina, then back again. "How are we going to get groceries up here?"

Frannie looked panicked for an instant and then with her most artful charm said, "Why, my dear, we'll just live on love."

Leonard looked bewildered.

Rina shepherded them forward. "We are there soon."

The pathway wound around the edge of the cliff, and above them, an old white plastered building sat nestled into the cliff as if it had always been there.

Rina bypassed the grand old wooden door in front of the building and approached a more modest metal-gated and more recent entrance.

Keys jangling in her hand. She glanced back at Frannie and Leonard. "This is…was a monastery but no more monks. Visitors, special visitors stay here."

Rina led the way into the old building honeycombed with passages and cells. Climbing upward Rina stopped in front of a narrow wooden door in an even narrower shadowy hallway that seemed to stretch on endlessly; door after wooden door on both sides.

Rina fumbled with the keys. She looked up at Frannie and Leonard. "We are here."

Leonard looked down the murky hallway skeptically.

Rina pushed the door open, revealing a shadowy apartment. She rushed to a large shuttered window. She opened a latch and threw open the shutters.

The whole wall of window came alive with glowing light. The low lying clouds, like huge galleons, sailed across the sky.

Frannie and Leonard stood transfixed. Rina moved two wooden chairs from a small wooden table and placed them right in front of the window. Grandly she waved at Frannie and Leonard. "Come sit down."

And they did.

November 22, 1996

> I had the strangest dream last night. I used to enjoy Dodo's dreams; they were so imaginative. My dreams were always more vague; they never seemed bright or real enough to tell anyone about them. It would ruin my image.
>
> But last night, I had a whooper of a dream, kind of horrible but interesting at the same time.

It must be these Italian beds or the crashing waves or even Leonard snoring next to me.

I was on a wagon train out west, you know, back when people rode in wagon trains. Time melted away a little like in my own life. Suddenly the whole wagon train party was sitting on the ground, tied up by the wagon wheels.

I heard screams in the distance. I realized in my dream that we had been captured by some tribal people and were being tortured one at a time. I also felt a little ashamed that we had been intruding on their land.

At this point in the dream, I realized that this was a dream. The screaming stopped for a minute, and I realized that the next person was taken away.

I struggled to wake up so that I could get out of the dream. I clicked my heels and moved my head, but I couldn't wake up, not for the life of me. I was terrified.

Suddenly from the distance or was it from inside, I heard this calm voice tolling like a deep bell. "Frannie, you can't wake up until you feel."

I woke up scared but also interested. I don't have a better word for it, just interested.

Her frizzy orange hair caught the spark of the Mediterranean sun as she sat, head down, the end of a pen in her mouth, absorbed in thought at a table in the busy piazza. She seemed as motionless as the statues at the fountain.

Slowly as if in some private trance, she gently set the pen down and gazed out into space. She started slightly as if something had intruded on her reverie. Warily she focused on something in the distance. Her whole body froze in place as if she was stalking some prey.

Leonard was cautiously walking, stepping out of the tunnel leading into the piazza. He took small steps as if he was walking through a minefield; funny how she had never noticed how frightened he seemed. His body appeared to be dragged by his head jutting forward, fiercely vigilant.

A small black dog scurried across the piazza, glanced over its shoulder at Leonard, then scurried even faster into a dark doorway. Leonard didn't notice.

He passed a stall where a handsome young man in tight new jeans was scooping gelato into a cup and handing it very cavalierly to a young woman who couldn't take her sad eyes off him. Leonard glanced at them, paused, wistfulness washing over his face, and once again continued his trip through the minefield. When he got to the center of the piazza, he stopped, perhaps sensing some impending danger. He saw Frannie looking directly at him, not unkindly but very intensely. He froze in place, like a deer in front of car headlights.

"Buon giorno, Leonardo." Frannie said with playful tenderness.

Leonard's face froze, his eyes wide with embarrassment. He glanced from side to side and then approached Frannie with those fast little inevitable steps of his. Embarrassment turned into his more usual hauteur. "Where were you all this time? I expected you back hours ago."

Frannie's playfulness melted away. For a second, she looked like a cornered animal, then her more usual cagey charm took over—the kind of charm that presumed the world would be entertained by her chance waywardness. "My dear, what a lovely surprise to see you. I love the romantic ring to Leonardo. Leonardo, I think I'll call you that from now on. Of course, we'll have to do something about that last name of yours."

Leonard clenched his jaw, and his eyes shone like hot coals.

Frannie's voice was becoming more strained sounding by the instant, but she kept up with her desperate banter. "How about Leonardo Fortunato?" Her voice began trailing off. "Such a lovely name, so artistic…"

Quite mechanically he pulled out the chair next to her and sat down. With quiet iciness, he said, "At least try not to make a scene. Why do you always have to make such a spectacle of yourself?"

A shakier Frannie looked down at the table. "I thought that you liked my scenes."

"When are you going to grow up?"

Frannie was very still, except that her hands were trembling slightly and a kind of shuddering seemed to be climbing up her spine.

When it reached her head, she snapped at him angrily. "At least I can be a child. You act like you were hatched out of some...reptile egg." As soon as she said it, she looked shocked at the words coming out of her.

Before her very eyes, Leonard morphed into a prosecuting attorney—cool, analytical, and going for the death penalty. "Do you hear how cruel and vindictive you are?"

He hit home; Analytical argument was not Frannie's strong suit, and she was even more susceptible to insult than to praise.

Her whole face turned an ugly red. After all, comforting men had been her raison d'être, and now she was accused of being a traitor. "I didn't mean...you know how I get carried away..."

Leonard had her; he knew it. He bent toward her, holding her eyes in a hammer lock. With a righteous wounded look on his face, he whispered, "You abuse me, Frannie. You've shown your true self, contemptuous and hateful."

Caught in his gaze, the last of her futile charm crumbled, leaving a confused and unappealing adolescent—the kind of teenager who spends too much time alone in basements, the kind of girl she had been.

With masterful condescension, he placed his hand on hers. Her eyes became red with ugly tears. "Now, Frannie, I chose you for better or worse."

Frannie looked up with the submission of someone who saw herself as clearly the worst.

He patted her hand.

She smiled obsequiously at him.

Leonard looked coldly matter-of-fact. "Now you have shopping to do for supper. And we'll pretend like this never happened."

They both got up in tandem, Leonard leading the way through the piazza.

About twenty feet from the table, Frannie stopped. Leonard glanced back at her with irritation. She ran back to the table and picked up her pad and pen. She picked them up and held them too her breast as if they were lost children. For an instant, she looked strangely sober and then flashed her most artful smile at Leonard. "You're such a dear to wait for me. Fish…we need fish tonight, something dark and mysterious that lives at the bottom of the bay." She bustled to his side.

CHAPTER 22

THE TWO TRUDGED back from town, carrying sacks of food, the solid form of Leonard leading the way; a few steps behind wafted Frannie in a parody of submission. She seemed engulfed more than usual in that abstract, almost dithering quality that people either loved or hated, following in her husband's wake. He turned around. Was that backward look a quick but bitter complaint or a desperate plea?

The crystal clear morning had smothered by ominous darkness; the sudden cold wind off the Mediterranean was hurling huge masses of dark wet clouds against the cliffs around the bay.

Leonard, much more solid, didn't seem at risk of the vicious wind, but Frannie, a mere red-haired wisp, seemed ready at any instant to take off in a sharp gust.

She paused, turning her head from the path toward the bay.

A ghostly fishing trawler with lights that pierced the gloom was slowly making its way far out beyond the bay scouring the depths for fish. She stood transfixed, absorbed by that silent and solitary search out there deeper than imagination. Those depths that seemed like some vast chaos, a place so dark, one dare not even contemplate, except on mornings like this when cliffs cut off hope of escape, and fancy was battered to salty loneliness. She took a deep breath, filling her lungs with the damp fishy smell on the wind.

She closed her eyes, but still the ocean rushed up against the gravelly beach. *Whoosh!* Then there was a moment of silence until the foamy water abandoned on shore retreated, whispering back over the stones to the sea that sent it. *Whoosh!* Another wave reached up for land until it could go no farther, then that instant of silence again, time caught and disappeared between the coming and going, leaving only a whisper behind. For a moment, she wondered if waves ever remember.

Her ears opened to the sounds that surrounded her. She was a mere point, barely visible, maybe not even that. Why, there was nothing for the wind to blow away. No one saw her, not even herself. The waves and her breath kept happening by themselves.

Once again, she opened her eyes, pointing herself toward Leonard; her feet began moving, joining with the wild rhythm.

Back with Leonard in the apartment, she spoke little, allowed herself to be folded in his embrace, and then cooked. She materialized just enough to give the impression of being present but not enough to take up space. Except for the cooking, that is. No wonder people love to cook.

She had bought a strange pink fish with delicate whiskers and glassy serious eyes. As soon as she had seen it at the fish store, she knew she wanted it for her guest this evening.

Like some sad-eyed Madonna, she lifted it out of the paper that it was wrapped in and held it gently. She washed the gaping wound in its stomach and laid the corpse out gently. Solemnly she dressed it with tomatoes and garlic and parsley, then placed it in the sepulcher of the frying pan. She turned the flame on underneath it and had one last silent moment of communion with that creature from the depths. She watched its eyes became silky white marbles and its flesh turn tender and flaky to the touch. Yes, she and the fish were transforming together—how marvelous to have a companion.

The raviolis were boiled in water as she sautéed fresh sage leaves in butter for the sauce, just like Rina had told her. In one last act of incredible daring and concentration, she threw strange green stalks of vegetable into boiling water. No hot dishes here; she thought she could see a glimmer of a smile on her sea companion in the pan.

With quiet presence, she pushed through the swinging door separating the tiny kitchen from the main room. Her face covered with a fine sheen of sweat and her hair damp like red seaweed, she carried in the steaming platter. She walked in front of the window and raised up the platter as if it was an offering to the darkness rushing and roaring outside.

The pink fish looked out with milky eyes as it lay on its bed of ravioli, ready for resurrection.

Leonard, sitting at the table, was clicking away on his desktop computer, paused as if for an instant; time had been snapped out from underneath him. He looked up fresh-faced at the strange sight before him.

She smiled easily and placed the platter on the table. "Supper is ready."

CHAPTER 23

November 23, 1996

The Amalfitini (that's what they call themselves) have started putting up little mangers in all the little piazzas—father, mother, child everywhere.

I started thinking about my father.

Yes, Dodo, I can see you nodding your head, smiling like an idiot, so proud of my newfound introspection. It wasn't just that Dad went away, but he started a whole new life that I wasn't part of.

He stopped visiting and calling; he even started forgetting my birthdays.

When I was fourteen, I spent one whole morning in the basement, looking through the box of pictures that my parents took when we were still a family together. I found some pictures where father and I were together, like on picnics or at Christmas.

One picture I especially loved was of him pushing me on a swing. I was laughing like I didn't have care in the world, and he was smiling at me as if he was proud. I loved that picture.

I bought a photo album and pasted those photos in it. I didn't tell Mom. Then I called him up and asked him if he could see me.

It was Christmastime. He sounded a little busy, but he said that he would meet me after school. I was a little nervous but very proud of what I had done. I suppose I thought that all he needed was a little reminding so that he would remember how he wanted to be with me.

When he picked me up that day, he said that he could only be with me a little while. He had to pick up his daughter from her dance lesson.

He had another daughter and a son. I didn't mind so much that he didn't have a present for me; after all, I called him on such short notice.

He opened my present and looked at the pictures. I thought that he would look happy, especially when he saw the swing picture, but he didn't.

He closed the book up. I knew that I shouldn't, but I asked him if he liked it. He looked out the window for a whole minute. Finally, he looked back at me like he was embarrassed, and he said that he had started a new life and that he didn't want to think about the old one.

He handed the album back to me. He wasn't mean or anything; he just didn't want to be reminded.

He dropped me off at my house with my photo album. I threw it in the trash. Mom might find it if I didn't get rid of it.

I could just see her noticing the pictures of my father and me. She would put her hands on her hips, begin tapping her toe against the linoleum floor, and say, "Now, Ms. High and Mighty, who do you think *you* are? What did he ever do for us?"

*   *   *

I had this strange experience yesterday afternoon.

Leonard was absorbed in his computer in the living room, and I was reading. He looked up at me, almost as if I were a stranger, and mentioned that he needed to take a bus into Salerno tomorrow; he needed to fax Thomas and Wanda. For a second, he looked sheepish. I said that if he didn't mind, I'd stay home. He looked relieved, and I felt relieved not to have to follow him around.

I walked into the kitchen. The apartment was still warm because it was early afternoon and sunny. For a moment, I just stood in the kitchen and looked at the red old-fashioned table with the bowl of fruit I had placed on it that morning. The way Leonard was in the other room and out of my mind, the way the afternoon sun came through the window and made the pears in the bowl seem warm and golden, alive, and hopeful, I sat down on one of the chairs right under the string of tomatoes that I had hung on the wall.

Rina showed me how to hang them. They are the small Italian tomatoes. You buy them still on the branches.

They look almost like berries. You can use them all winter. They don't exactly dry out completely, but they gradually shrivel a little, and the tomato juice inside becomes tangier and sweeter as time goes on.

So I sat down under them while the bells from town were ringing.

Then and there I just knew that I was actually sitting in the kitchen. I know that sounds silly; I have sat in this kitchen many times since moving into the apartment, but I never actually knew I was here—HERE with capital letters.

I could feel the warmth of the sun. I could smell the tomatoes getting tangier, but most of all, I was surrounded by sound.

I knew that I was really here because sound was all around me, a car whirring and rattling on the road down below along the bay, two children running up the stairs, their rapidly clopping feet echoing in the canyon of the stairwell, and the sound of someone sweeping the floor above. *Shshsh, shshsh, shshsh*! I swear that I could hear the sound of the cliffs above slowly disintegrating into the fine dust that coated everything in the apartment.

I reached for a pear and felt my hand move through the air. I was reaching for the pear all of me.

Everything else from the morning before seemed like a dream. I touched the pear and picked it up. Oh, how warm and soft it felt, yielding to the pressure of my fingers flesh to flesh.

I took a paring knife from the tray by the sink and ever so slowly pressed the blade to the yellow skin, and all the time, I was swimming in the sounds and warmth all around me almost dizzy.

I angled the knife and pressed it to the skin. I heard a soft grainy sound as the blade sliced through. I was so surprised by the sound that the pear and I made; I started giggling until I felt the pear throbbing. Was it in pain? As if in answer, beads of liquid began weeping from the naked flesh, but instead of bitter salty tears they were sweet and fresh like a beautiful morning.

Tears started to come from my eyes too, and like the pears, they were sweet, not bitter.

FRANNIE SAT AT a little table on the piazza, the sky a tentative blue, the town alive with smells and sounds, and people pulsed around her. Her eyes, red-rimmed, looked at her notepad.

"Ciao, Frannie." Rina, sunglasses on, stepped out of the commotion in the piazza.

Frannie looked up, fresh, slightly bewildered as if she had just woken up from a peaceful sleep.

Rina, a concerned look on her face, took off her sunglasses as she walked up to the table. "Are you feeling…how are you feeling?"

"Oh, I was lost in thought, maybe not even in thought. Have you ever had so much happen that you just kind of start drifting out?"

"Lost…in…thought." Rina was concentrating, repeating the words slowly as if they were a puzzle that she was figuring out. Finally, she looked at Frannie. "Lost in thought. I like that. Sometimes I get lost…in Naples or up in hills. Yes, I get lost in thoughts also. After my divorce, I get lost in thought."

"I didn't know you were divorced. I didn't know anybody got divorced in Italy."

"I divorced one year ago. People divorce in Italy but not Amalfi."

"That must have been terribly difficult."

"Yes, but we do not talk about men now." As Rina sat down, she waved to a familiar waiter, and he placed a small cup of espresso in front of her. A thin wedge of lemon floated in the thick brown mixture. She smelled it for a moment and took a sip, nodding at Frannie for no particular reason. "We put lemon in coffee…Amalfi way."

"My, I never heard of that before. I have always drunk mine with milk. It reminds me of the cocoa I had as a child."

"You try?"

For an instant, Frannie looked doubtful, even a little shocked, then her face warmed into an excited smile. "I try."

Rina waved at the waiter. "*Cafe con limone per favore.*" She pointed to Frannie.

The waiter brought a tiny cup of coffee.

The two women stopped talking for a moment.

Then quite proprietarily Rina said, "Cafe con limone, Frannie."

Frannie picked up the little cup carefully and brought it up to her lips. She smelled the thick roasted smell of coffee, but then she noticed the subtle twist of something sharp and flowery. Why, it was that little slice of floating lemon.

She pressed the cup to her lips. The heavy taste of coffee melted into her mouth, rich and almost grainy, and then she tasted the delicate reminder of lemon. "Why, I don't even need milk and sugar with my coffee. This is really wonderful. I like the way you do things in Italy. You put things together in different ways. Everything is so mixed up here."

"Mixed up? What means mixed up? Like *pazzo*?"

"Pazzo?"

"Pazzo like how you say *crazy*?"

"Oh no, not like that. That wouldn't be a very nice thing to say. I mean mixed up in a good way. When a bunch of different kinds of things are all mixed together, like that fountain over there. There's a man being tortured to death while that girl with water shooting out of her breasts is smiling. That sort of thing. I always thought that things could only happen one at a time."

Rina seemed to be listening very carefully, nodding her head occasionally. "I like mixed up, Frannie." Rina seemed serious for a moment, and then they both silently began sipping their coffee.

Frannie glanced up toward the tower. "How do people get up there?"

"There are many places, paths where people walk up cliff." Rina looked up beaming at Frannie. "We go now?"

Frannie looked embarrassed as if she had somehow broken a rule. "I can't take you away."

Rina smiled. "You must see tower."

The two women walked down an alley that Frannie had never noticed before. Streets have a way of tunneling through Amalfi, upstairs, down dark passages, in back of wonderful smelling kitchens, under lines of laundry, and through hidden courtyards. They are not really streets but paths through the plastered layered organism called Amalfi, an organism that has managed to thrive on this unlikely place for many hundreds of years.

When the Roman Empire was collapsing in one of those remembered moments of Italy, Roman exiles found this place—a place so impossibly preposterous that they could set up a little empire on the rocks and narrow beach untouched by the barbaric chaos that ravaged the rest of Europe.

As Frannie walked through the paths, she was walking through layers of history through a collective memory: Roman columns supporting the walls of a baroque church and houses where a modern kitchen looked out the windows formed by medieval arches. Even the people seemed mixed up: teenagers in the latest designer jeans and old women in black dresses that women have worn here for centuries. So much memory here and everywhere lemons.

The two women walked up a particularly steep tunnel. In the gloom was a shrine to a sad-eyed Madonna looking ever so much like a stately goddess. Someone had left a tiny bouquet of snapdragons by the candle that flickered Frannie's shadows across the walls. She didn't really know what would pop out of this strange world around her.

They entered a dark passageway; a brilliant apparition light shone at its end.

As they stepped out of the tunnel, her eyes blurred with the sudden brilliance. They were standing above the town. The white roofs gleamed, and dark forms pursued the everyday life between the buildings—an everyday life that they had been going on for ages. And she was hanging above it all surrounded by the lemon groves.

She heard water dripping and looked up to see drops of water trickling from a limestone overhang right above her. The drops made little splashing sounds in a tiny pool by the path.

Some soft ferns hung over the shaded damp. Though she had always hated heights, she looked up and out toward the sea. The turquoise stretched out beneath her just beyond Amalfi; stretching out it seemed forever until it merged with the blue of the sky.

She had a sudden spinning feeling as the sea spreading out below seemed to lurch up and tilt pouring itself into sky. She closed her eyes, and even her senses were mixed up. She could hear the greens and blues all around her coming from everywhere, and she felt the sound of the dripping water like time.

"Are you feel all right, Frannie?"

Frannie slowly opened her eyes cautiously. "I just felt dizzy all of a sudden. I know it's silly. I felt that I was on the edge of the world, and it was starting to tilt. At any moment, I might spin out into all the blue. Funny, isn't it? I don't know if I was afraid of falling or afraid sailing off forever."

Rina smiled at her. "We sit down here. We rest and look."

"Oh, I hate to be such a baby!"

"You sit down." Rina gestured toward a small bench by the pool.

The two sat down in the shade of the cliff. "There that does feels better."

Rina studied her for an instant. "We go to tower now."

They set off on the path, winding up to the dark tower. They passed around a steep mass of rock that blocked out the sea and sun. In shadow, they walked up the last steep incline. A huge stone wall surrounded the peak of the hill and the duchess's tower that seemed to point ominously upward.

As Frannie got closer, she realized that the wall was a ruin, the path leading through a gaping whole. For a moment, she could almost hear horses and swords clanging and terrible screams; she stepped through the gap in the wall revealing sunlight grass.

The tower stood oddly serene on that knoll despite its terrible memories. A bird song thrilled the blue sky; she could feel the sun on her face and could hear the whispering of the sea.

Frannie paused…delight after horror. Rina turned around and waved Frannie forward with tender humor.

Rina and Frannie stepped through a break in the tower wall and quite suddenly were inside the top of the tower.

Time or tragedy or both had torn away the whole upper section of the tower, leaving the memories free to fly out and join all the other stories of sadness and joy that fill the Italian skies.

Rina and Frannie sat on a piece of collapsed stonework, the blue sky their ceiling.

Rina waved her arm up at the sky. "See, the duchess, she's free."

CHAPTER 24

LEONARD WALKED WITH halting steps down the narrow streets of Salerno, old stone buildings squeezed the road ever tighter; women sitting in shadowy doorways; and motor scooters roaring, darting past the shiny shop windows each more enticing trays of ravioli, leather jackets, or pastries on parade.

Leonard seemed oblivious, even vague, glancing reluctantly at whatever jarring stimulus intruded and then returning to his uneasy reverie. His head, usually standing look out on the mast of his body ever straining forward watching for danger in the distance, was now nested on his shoulders preoccupied with his internal drama. He ran into a cart of vegetables in that narrow road, brushed his pants off, and kept walking while the stubble-faced man in a dirty apron behind the cart watched him disapproving amazement.

On the other side of that canyon of a street, an old woman in a third floor window was pulling up a basket of groceries on a rope while a young boy watched from underneath.

Triggered by some internal purpose, he stopped in front of a small open café. A middle-aged man and woman standing at the counter drinking coffee interrupted their argument and starred at the apparition of Leonard stalled in front of them. The elegantly dressed young man behind the counter glanced in Leonard's direction and turned back to press a lever on his magnificent espresso machine.

As the steam hissed and roared, rising to the ceiling, Leonard snapped out of his fugue glancing nervously at the wooden telephone stalls next to the steaming counter. His head once again jutting forward, he looked from side to side as if he was afraid someone might be watching and slipped into one of the booths as secretly as a spy. The splendid espresso machine stopped roaring, and the middle-aged couple started once again to argue.

Leonard stood motionless inside the booth, feeling the sweat trickle from his armpits down his side. His hand darted into his pocket; he pulled out a crumpled piece of paper. His eyes wide with excitement, his hands shaking, he opened it as if it was a treasure map.

Wanda's name and phone number was revealed on that scrap of paper. He stared at it once again stalling. He took a deep breath and, with determination renewed, reached into his other pocket pulling out a handful of jangling coins.

He picked up the receiver and began drooping those coins one at a time into the slot on the telephone. With each coin dropping and chiming, his excitement seemed be stoked further.

By the time the receiver started ringing, he looked like a desperately thrilled and devious boy. One ring…two rings…his eyes widened and teeth clenched…three rings…any moment he looked like he would explode with tension…four rings, and the sound of an answering service switched on. "This is Wanda Reilly of Celebrations Unlimited, the first choice for all your party needs…" He banged the receiver down and closed his eyes. For an instant, he was in a nowhere land. He opened his eyes and crumbled the piece of paper in his fist.

Pale and lost-looking, he stepped out of the booth. All three people at the counter watched him. He looked down in embarrassment.

In good-natured broken English, the waiter said, "You call your sweetheart?"

Leonard stood there, a boy caught in the act, and to no one in particular, he said, "I was just contacting a business colleague… nothing personal." He fled the bar.

As he scrambled down the street, he tried to create a facsimile of his former self…pace steady and mechanical, head jutting forward, vigilant and single-minded. He stiffened his back, and his face froze over with its normal hauteur. That's better, walking the street, master of the world or at least of Grimbaugh and associates.

He turned at the intersection onto a broader street with shinier shop windows, cars going by at a more regular pace. What *is* that clanging sound?

He looked up ahead. A flat piece of metal was lying insolently in the left lane of the street. Each car—front wheel, then back wheel— rolled over it, clanging again and again. In the rhythm of racket, his feet seemed to periodically falter ever so slightly, and though his face still looked imposing, there was just hint of indecision around his mouth. But his eyes, something about his eyes, a ghost of something lingered there. For assurance, he glanced at himself in a store window and saw a stranger.

CHAPTER 25

IN THE DARK bedroom, they huddled, two big lumps, facing away from each other, spaced as far apart as the bed would permit.

Outside the night wind was driving the waves in the bay crazy, splattering ran against the window. One particularly determined gust of wind stormed the window with an explosive thrust, rattled the whole window violently.

Leonard, the larger lump facing the window, stirred. He half-turned toward the lump on the far side of the bed, then turned back toward the murky chaos on the other side of the glass. Just as he seemed to be settling in again, the windowpane exploded again with sudden fury. His eyes opened wide, and in the sickly glow of the storm, for the life of him, he looked lost.

Frannie, the other lump, turned on her back. Leonard turned in her direction, and that lump of himself slowly but irrevocable edged toward her. She could feel the slowly approaching warmth of him.

The window rattled frantically again; he clutched her around the waist like a life preserver. She opened her eyes, just lying there, staring out into the darkness, listening to the smashing waves, and feeling Leonard's urgent arm around her waist.

Her voice joined into the night's commotion. "Are you all right, dear?"

No sound but just the hint of a tremor in that form pressing against her.

She took a slightly deeper than usual breath, a thoughtful breath, and continued to stare up at the ceiling.

His hand reached for her breast.

She stirred. "Has it been a hard trip?"

Still huddled against her. "I hate storms."

As if taunted by his dread, the window rattled again.

She gently took the hand that had been clutching at her breast and cradled it in both her hands. Her voice was gentle but ironic. "We're quite a pair you and I."

That lump of Leonard struggled under the covers.

Frannie held his hand firmly.

"It wasn't supposed to be this way."

"I know."

"I want things to be the way they were."

A moment of silence, waves crashing below, she turned toward him. "All the kings' horses and all the kings' men couldn't put Humpty together again."

His body seemed to freeze solid, and then he suddenly jerked up on his elbow, glaring angrily at her. The frightened boy disappeared. The whole bed rocked crazily. "Making fun of me! You ought to be ashamed of yourself." He glared down at her.

For an instant, her eyes opened wide in fear, then slowly her face began to relax. Her eyes fastened onto to his, but there was a funny kind of quiet behind them if she was focusing on something inside instead of out.

Slowly her lips opened, the words soft but not placating. "I said *we* were quite a pair." She kept him in her direct gaze.

At first, he looked like some bewildered animal just discovering that he was trapped. Was that terror on his face?

She smiled, a strange kind of smile. "I'm Humpty, and you're Dumpty, and here we are landed in Amalfi."

The wind pounded the glass frantically. He startled; the little boy peeking out again.

She started laughing.

He watched her. Then something like an embarrassed smile snuck up on him.

Her eyes coaxed his.
He smiled.
She smiled back.

CHAPTER 26

THROUGH THE BROAD window of the Cracked Cup, the worn street outside looked almost fresh. Skinny trees along the boulevard were just breaking out into new leaves—that glowing light green color of long-promised spring days.

Frannie and Dwayne walked along the sidewalk outside, talking a mile a minute.

The door swung open; Frannie stepped in followed by Dwayne. She paused, studying the room, and the usual cast of misfits huddled around tables drinking coffee. She smiled, glad to be home.

Dwayne grinned at her. "Hello, Dolly."

Frannie snapped her imaginary castanets and twirled in a full circle. No one in the room looked up.

Dwayne shrugged his shoulders. "Maybe they didn't know you were gone."

Frannie pantomimed shock, then she shrugged her shoulders and winked at Dwayne.

Those two road warriors, in fine form, headed over to the counter. A rather bored-looking young woman with two pigtails sprouting out of her head interrupted her conversation with a young skinny guy wearing a tight black suit, long enough to eye the two middle-aged people coolly. She went back to her conversation with the young man.

Dwayne glared at her.

Slowly still keeping up her conversation, she edged in Frannie and Dwayne's direction. Almost by accident, she found herself standing in front of the two, still engrossed in her conversation.

Dwayne's irritation softened into wistfulness as he looked over at Frannie. "Do you remember how it felt when everybody noticed us?"

Frannie shook her head in mock outrage.

Half angry, half humorously Dwayne bent over the counter and stuck his face right next to the young woman's face. "I'm the amazing invisible man." He laughed maniacally.

She focused on him in total surprise. "Oh yeah, what do you want?"

"This person— he points to Frannie grandly—"is the last queen of Albania, living in relative but tasteful obscurity, waiting for her summons back to the throne."

The young woman glanced coolly at Frannie. "Right." She turned back to Dwayne. "What do you want?"

"We'll have our usual."

The young woman looked bewildered.

He glanced over at Frannie. "They forget so soon." He turned back to the young woman, relenting. "I'll have the depth charge, and her highness will have a latte with plenty of foam."

Frannie cocked her head, watching the two combatants. She smiled at the young woman with absolute candor and said, "When you grow older, sometimes it is a little hard to let younger people take center stage."

The young woman looked at Frannie with some interest.

Very confidentially Frannie bent a little closer to the young woman. "I would like to try something different today."

The young woman echoed, "Different?"

Frannie confided, "When I was in Italy, a friend there taught me another way to have coffee. You take a cup of espresso and float a thin slice of lemon in it." She looks over at Dwayne. "Would you like to try it?"

He looked at her askance. "Lemon in my coffee? I never mix fruit and beans. It gives me gas."

The young woman frowned at Dwayne. "You're not just invisible. You don't try new things either?"

"Okay, okay."

The young woman turned back to the shiny espresso machine.

Above the roar of the steam, Dwayne smiled at Frannie. "I missed you. Life seems so dreary sometimes. Even when I do everything right."

Frannie looked at him tenderly and then laughed. "At least I've never been accused of doing everything right."

The waitress turned around with three cups of espresso. She grabbed a clear glass half full of lemon slices. She handed it to Frannie.

Frannie took a spoon and picked out a lemon slice and very gently laid in them in the steaming espresso cups.

All eyes are focused on Frannie. "Give it a little time to float there. Isn't that lovely?" Her eyes gleamed as bright as spring leaves.

"Now you can pick up your cup. Smell it. That's it. Isn't that wonderful! Now you can taste it one little sip at a time. Don't rush it. Do you notice how the thick roasted taste of the coffee mixes with the thin clear taste of lemon? Remarkable, isn't it?"

May 3, 1997

Such a quiet evening, Leonard clicking away at his computer in the next room and minding his own business.

After talking with Mona for what seemed like forever, I turned on the TV.

One of those nature shows was playing on public television. There staring out at me from the screen was this big red-haired orangutan, just sitting up on that tree, staring out. It seemed so part of everything.

Even though its jungle could be cleared tomorrow, for that moment, it sat there belonging.

The end

CPSIA information can be obtained
at www.ICGtesting.com
Printed in the USA
BVHW081154270922
648083BV00002B/285

9 781648 957291